Underground Railroad

Produced by the
Division of Publications
National Park Service

U.S. Department of the Interior
Washington, D.C.

In 1990, Congress directed the Secretary of the Interior acting through the Director of the National Park Service to conduct a study of alternatives for commemorating and interpreting the Underground Railroad, the approximate routes taken by enslaved fugitives escaping to freedom before the conclusion of the Civil War. The Congress also directed the Secretary of the Interior acting through the Director of the National Park Service to prepare and publish an interpretive handbook on the Underground Railroad in the larger context of American Antebellum society, including the history of slavery and abolitionism. This handbook has been prepared by the National Park Service in fulfillment of our charge under Public Law 101-628. It is my hope that the reading and discussion of our shared past will benefit all Americans.

The Underground Railroad story is like nothing else in American history: a secret enterprise that today is famous, an association many claim but few can document, an illegal activity now regarded as noble, a network that was neither underground nor a railroad, yet a system that operated not with force or high finance but through the committed and often spontaneous acts of courage and kindness of individuals unknown to each other. Perhaps the Underground Railroad lives in America's consciousness because it serves so many myths and challenges so many others. For all Americans in search of a shared past, it proves that brutal systems and brutal laws can be overturned from within. It demonstrates that people can struggle and free themselves from bondage through individual and collective acts of courage. It speaks of the power of freedom and justice.

This is an amazing story and a timely one that offers insight into America's need to face our collective history together and recreate our past with each generation. This handbook which draws together court records, buildings, letters, and memories and draws on the research of historians tells the story anew. The Underground Railroad has a special place in our nation's historic memory. The National Park Service is committed to assuring that this history will be preserved. We invite your participation.

Robert Stanton
Director, National Park Service

A desperate Margaret Garner pleads in vain with slave catchers in Cincinnati, Ohio, where she, her husband, and four children had fled from Kentucky. Accounts and illustrations of what happened vary, but in 1856 Garner reportedly killed one child and wounded three in an attempt to prevent their recapture. She was sold back into slavery in the Deep South, where she died of typhoid fever in 1858.

An Epic in United States History

Myth and Reality

By Larry Gara

The intriguing story of the Underground Railroad is one of America's great legends, a mix of historical facts embroidered with myths. Traditionally the term refers to a multitude of routes to freedom taken by fugitive slaves. Typically the story focuses primarily on abolitionist operators and pictures fugitives as helpless, frightened passengers. The story, told in the context of a free North and a slaveholding South, often assumes that only by taking advantage of a well-organized national network of abolitionists could slaves have succeeded in escaping. Numerous accounts tell of daring rescues, ingenious underground hiding places, and tunnels connecting nearby rivers to underground stations.

In fact, however, the North before the Civil War was not entirely free, either. By the end of the American Revolutionary era all Northern states had abolished slavery or had made provision to do so, but fugitive slaves were always in danger of being returned under federal law and, in some cases, even under state law. Consequently, after Britain abolished slavery throughout its colonies in 1833, Canada became an important destination for fugitives who feared recapture and return to bondage. The Fugitive Slave Law of 1850, which greatly expanded federal powers to protect the interests of slaveholders, posed a new threat to all fugitives in Northern states, and large numbers fled to Canada. Many stories about the Underground Railroad grew from events after passage of that law.

Ironically, while the 1850 law mandated Northern involvement in the return of fugitive slaves, it also led many Northerners to become moderate antislavery sympathizers. They already resented the power granted to the South in the U.S. Constitution whereby slaveholding states were allowed to count every five slaves as three persons for purposes of Congressional representation and the assignment of electoral votes. It was that power rather than slavery itself that many Northerners resented. The new law requiring that slaves be returned fueled anger and opposition to Southern demands.

This passageway (enlarged since the Underground Railroad era) at the Milton House Inn in Milton, Wisconsin, is locally believed to have been used by fugitive slaves.
Inside front cover: *A page from Quaker Daniel Osborn's 1844 diary lists fugitive slaves passing through the Alum Creek Settlement in Ohio.*
Pages 4-5: *A black couple flees with their child to the relative safety of Union lines near Manassas, Virginia, in Eastman Johnson's 1862 painting,* A Ride for Liberty: The Fugitive Slaves.

The mythical Underground Railroad became best known after the Civil War, but it had its roots in the antebellum period. Both abolitionists and defenders of slavery dealt in exaggeration; it was not a time in which individuals stuck to cold facts. Abolitionists boasted of their aid to fugitive slaves or announced their willingness to give such aid. Fugitive slaves like Frederick Douglass were effective spokespersons for abolition and often were featured speakers at antislavery gatherings. Stories like that of Shadrach Minkins, a fugitive who was rescued from jail in Boston and sent on to Canada, got national attention and helped generate sympathy for slaves who had the courage and ingenuity to leave the South.

For their part, Southern politicians exaggerated the number of escapes and blamed them all on Northerners interfering with Southern property rights. Because of exaggeration and the lack of proper record keeping, numbers of escapes cannot be exact. While it is clear that there were more than the thousand annual slave escapes listed in census returns, any approximate number would fall far short of the total of one million suggested by several persons.

Because few contemporary documents concerning the Underground Railroad have survived, most of the sources are autobiographical accounts written years after the events occurred. The abolitionist memoirs are based on recollections of members of a much-reviled minority writing after they had seen their cause triumph and their years of loyal service vindicated. While they vary in authenticity, most tend to relate events from one point of view. Little or nothing was written about the ingenious and daring escape plans carried out by the fugitives themselves. The exception was *The Underground Railroad* written in 1872 by William Still, an African American. He published numerous documents, including his own interviews with fugitives who were going through Philadelphia, and focused attention on what he referred to as the "self-emancipated champions" of his race.

In the years after the Civil War, stories about the Underground Railroad appeared in magazines and newspapers. Many of these accounts were based on the memories of aging abolitionists and embellished by reporters. Through such tales the Underground Railroad entered the realm of American folklore. Even those close to the events had difficulty separating fact

from fiction. Gary Collison's biography of Shadrach Minkins tells of conflicting and erroneous rumors and myths concerning Shadrach's brief stay in Concord, Massachusetts, on his way to Canada.

In the postwar years such terms as "passenger" and "conductor" of the Underground Railroad received wide circulation. What were only cellars, servants' quarters, and storage rooms were assumed to have been constructed for hiding fugitive slaves. Legendary material was repeated in stories, novels, plays, and even historical monographs. In 1898 Professor Wilbur H. Siebert published the classic history, *The Underground Railroad from Slavery to Freedom*, which he based on correspondence with descendants and others claiming knowledge of the institution. His collection is valuable, but some stories he accepted could not be verified.

While there were always some individuals willing to provide food and shelter to fleeing slaves, the term Underground Railroad did not come into common use until the construction of actual railroads became widespread. In 1844 an abolitionist newspaper in Chicago published a cartoon captioned "The Liberty Line" that portrayed happy fugitives in a railroad car going to Canada from the United States. Passage of the Fugitive Slave Law of 1850 also led to more common use of the term and to increased aid to fugitive slaves.

The African Meeting House in Boston dates to 1806 and is the oldest surviving black church in the United States. Today it is a part of Boston African American National Historic Site, which includes 15 pre-Civil War structures linked by a Black Heritage Trail. The Mother Bethel A.M.E. Church, shown below in an 1820s lithograph, was at the center of the antislavery movement in Philadelphia.

The popular myth depicts a nationwide, centralized underground operation. One novelist pictures a highly organized, smooth-running operation with stations in both the North and the South, all of it masterminded by an elderly, invalid Quaker woman. In truth, there was some organized activity in certain localities, but none nationwide. Much of the aid to fugitives was haphazard. One or two incidents concerning fugitive slaves could give a community a reputation for a thriving system of aid. Local pride contributed to the popularity of the myth as unverified family stories appeared in local historical publications.

Inevitably, a good deal of exaggeration entered the picture. At least four communities claimed to be the place where the term Underground Railroad originated, and at least five individuals were referred to in postwar accounts as "president" of the Underground Railroad. While some abolitionists had well-deserved reputations for their work with fugitive slaves, many individuals who had little or no record of such service but who had held moderate to strong antislavery views were assumed, after the war, to have been part of the Underground Railroad.

Legendary accounts tend to blur the many divisions within the antislavery movement. While many Quakers supported Underground Railroad activities, others opposed what they viewed as extremist ideas. In the 1840s, Free-Soilers who favored only political measures that restricted slavery to the South had little to do with the fugitive slave issue, but after the Civil War many were associated with it in Underground Railroad stories.

One of the more persistent myths concerns tunnels or underground hiding places. One story, frequently repeated, described such a tunnel under St. John's Episcopal Church in Cleveland, Ohio. The Western Reserve Historical Society conducted two separate investigations that concluded no such tunnels ever existed. In 1993 Byron D. Fruehling made on-site investigations of seventeen Ohio houses reputed to have had some kind of subterranean hiding places for fugitive slaves. He concluded that even though some of the buildings may have housed escaping slaves in antebellum years, the fugitives hid in barns, attics, or spare rooms, not in underground hideaways.

Another myth is that absolute secrecy was necessary in all Underground Railroad operations. Abolitionists such as Levi Coffin, William Still, and Thomas Garrett made no secret of their work aiding fugitives. Of these three only Garrett, who lived in Delaware, a border slave state, was arrested under the Fugitive Slave Law. Obviously there were times when such activities had to be carried out in secret, but reputations of abolitionists generally were well known.

The legend of the Underground Railroad has taken on a life of its own and become a major epic in American history. It recalls a time when white and black abolitionists worked unselfishly together in the cause of human freedom. Like all legends it is oversimplified, whereas historical reality is complex. Sorting out fact from fiction is the everyday work of historians. In the next section of this book, two historians summarize their current conclusions in essays about slavery and the Underground Railroad.

1565

African slaves arrive on North American mainland at Spanish colony of St. Augustine.

1619

Africans arrive in Virginia on Dutch ship; slave trade intensifies in latter part of 17th century.

1760s

Charles Mason and Jeremiah Dixon survey Pennsylvania-Maryland boundary; in time, this marks division between slave and free states.

1770

Crispus Attucks is killed by British soldiers in the Boston Massacre.

1775

First abolition society forms in Philadelphia.

1793

Congress passes first Fugitive Slave Law affirming Constitutional rights of slaveholders to their property.

1808

United States abolishes trade in slaves from Africa.

1831

Nat Turner leads slave insurrection in Virginia.

1833

William Lloyd Garrison heads New England Anti-Slavery Society; Margaretta Forten forms Female Anti-Slavery Society in Philadelphia; British Parliament passes Emancipation Act freeing all slaves and outlawing the slave trade.

1830s

Vigilance committees organize in Northern cities to prevent return of fugitive slaves to the South.

1839

Slaves revolt on Spanish ship *Amistad* off Cuba.

1845

Frederick Douglass's first autobiography is published.

1850

Fugitive Slave Law requires escapees be returned; Harriet Tubman begins helping slaves escape via Underground Railroad.

Harriet Tubman (1823–1913) nurse, spy and scout

135,000 SETS, 270,000 VOLUMES SOLD.

UNCLE TOM'S CABIN

FOR SALE HERE.

AN EDITION FOR THE MILLION, COMPLETE IN 1 Vol., PRICE 12 CENTS.
" " IN GERMAN, IN 1 Vol., PRICE 50
" " IN 2 Vols. CLOTH, 6 PLATES, PRICE
SUPERB ILLUSTRATED EDITION, IN 1 Vol., WITH 153 ENGRAVINGS,
PRICES FROM $2.50 TO

The Greatest Book of the Age.

1852
Harriet Beecher Stowe's *Uncle Tom's Cabin* published.

1854
Kansas-Nebraska Act allows territories to choose to be slave or free states.

1857
U.S. Supreme Court's Dred Scott Decision rules that free blacks and slaves are not citizens.

1859
Abolitionist John Brown raids U.S. Armory at Harpers Ferry.

1860
Republican Abraham Lincoln wins U.S. Presidential election in November; South Carolina secedes from Union in December.

1861
Civil War begins as Confederates attack Fort Sumter in April; Union declares fugitive slaves as contraband of war in May.

1862
Lincoln signs bill in April abolishing slavery in District of Columbia and providing funds for voluntary colonizations; in May Congress prohibits slavery in territories; in July the Second Confiscation Act permits military to enlist blacks.

1863
Lincoln's Emancipation Proclamation takes effect, abolishing slavery in Confederacy; Union intensifies recruitment of blacks as soldiers.

1865
Civil War ends in April; Lincoln assassinated; Thirteenth Amendment to U.S. Constitution outlawing slavery ratified in December.

From Bondage to Freedom

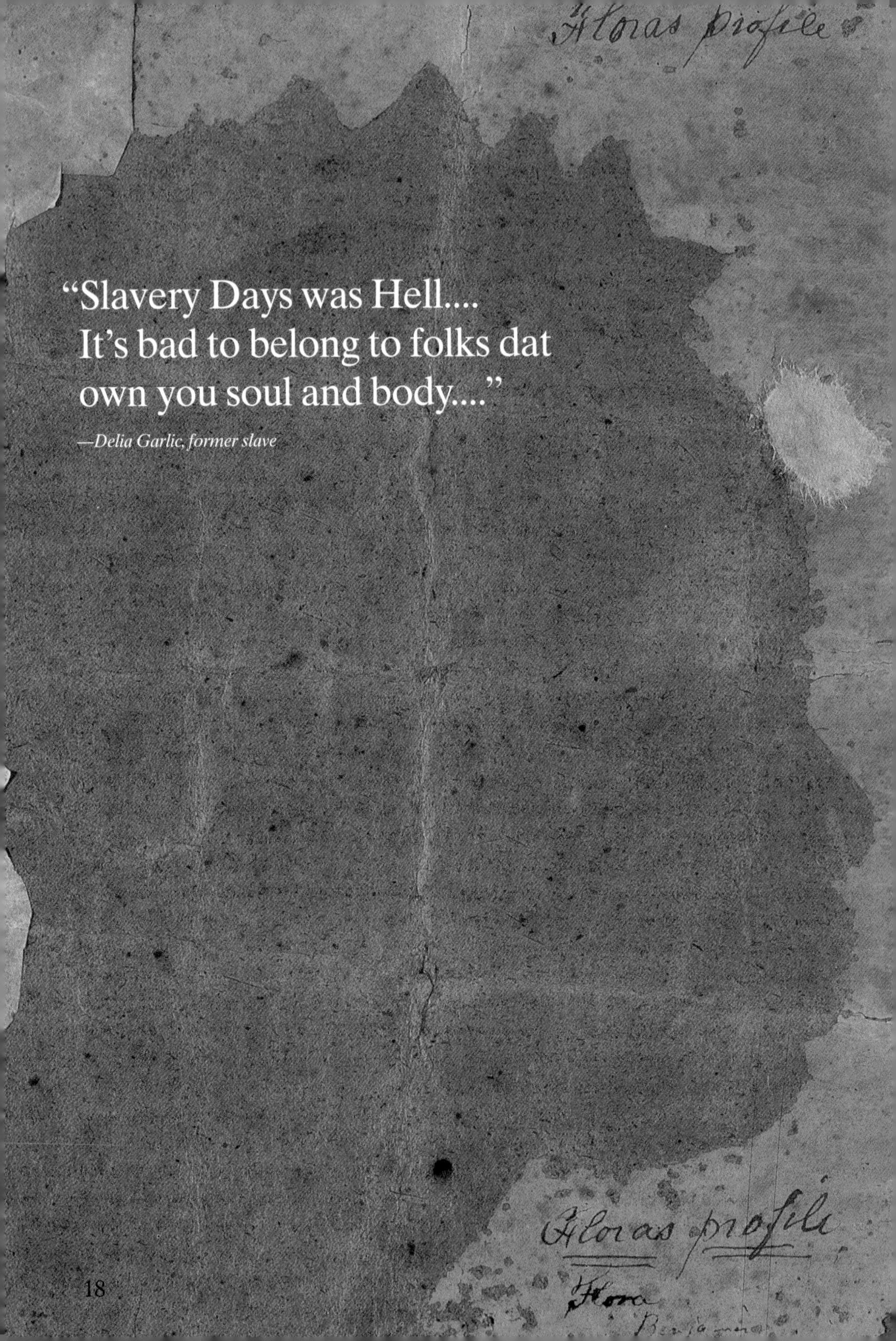

"Slavery Days was Hell....
It's bad to belong to folks dat
own you soul and body...."

—*Delia Garlic, former slave*

Floras profile

Floras profile

Flora
Benjamin

18

Slavery in America

By Brenda E. Stevenson

Slavery, the institution and the people who were part of it, has had tremendous and long-lasting influence on American history and the American people. Common perceptions of the slaves and slaveholders, shrouded in mythology almost from the beginning, have changed dramatically over time. But lingering notions of Southern difference and black inferiority—both intimately linked to slavery—still remain along with a host of related questions about race and democracy. To study the history of slavery in the United States, therefore, is also to explore some of the fundamental questions that confront Americans of every generation.

Africans came with the first Europeans to the Americas in exploratory and exploitative missions as seamen, pirates, workers, and slaves. Scholars have documented the presence of Africans on the expeditions of Columbus to the Caribbean, Cortez to Mexico, Narváez in Florida, Cabeza de Vaca in the American Southwest, Hawkins in Brazil, Balboa in the Pacific, Pizarro in Peru, DeSoto in the North American Southeast, and Jesuit missionaries in Canada.

The first Africans designated as slave laborers arrived in the Caribbean in 1518. A century later, the first blacks were brought to Jamestown, Virginia, where, for the next few decades, they were given a status similar to that of indentured servants.

Initially Europeans brought only small numbers of Africans to the New World. However, as the need for labor grew with expansions in agriculture, mining, and other businesses, so, too, did the number of black slaves. Brazil and the Caribbean had the largest numbers of imports and for the longest span of time, with Brazil and Cuba maintaining importation until the 1880s. Figures are imprecise, but over the period Brazil received at least 4 million slaves; the French Caribbean, 1.6 million; the Dutch Caribbean, 0.5 million; the English Caribbean, 1.8 million; the Spanish Caribbean and mainland colonies, 1.6 million; and those British mainland colonies, subsequently the United States, 450,000.

Gradual emancipation in the North did not free all slaves. This bill of sale states that a 19-year-old slave named Flora, depicted at left in an accompanying cut-paper silhouette, was sold for £25 in 1796 by Margaret Dwight to Asa Benjamin in Connecticut. Flora died in

1815. As with most slaves, little is known about her life, but more than likely she would have agreed with Delia Garlic's comment about slavery.
Preceding pages: *Jerry Pinkney's illustration evokes the caution and watchfulness that accompanied a successful flight from bondage.*

Atlantic Slave Trade

The slave trade across the Atlantic followed a long history of trade in people and goods between Europe, Asia, and Africa. Rivalries among European powers in the 1500s and 1600s sparked rapid exploitation of the New World's mineral and agricultural resources and initiated an intense and destructive period of bonded labor in the Americas. Africans were traded, purchased, or captured to work the gold and silver mines of South and Central America and the sugar plantations of the Caribbean.

Under pressure from European traders—first Spanish and Portuguese, later Dutch, English, and some French—the social fabric and trade economy of West and Central Africa changed. Since Africans were producers and frequently exporters of cloth, ornaments, and iron products, the Europeans' most valued trade goods were guns, which were then used in wars to acquire slaves. Of the approximate 10 million Africans shipped to the Western Hemisphere, only 450,000 were taken to what is now the United

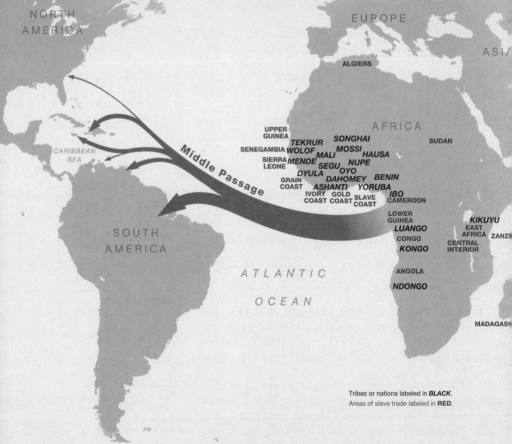

NORTH AMERICA

EUROPE

ASIA

ALGIERS

AFRICA

UPPER GUINEA
TEKRUR   SONGHAI   SUDAN
SENEGAMBIA WOLOF   MOSSI
SIERRA MENDE MALI   HAUSA
LEONE   SEGU NUPE
        DYULA   OYO
GRAIN   DAHOMEY BENIN
COAST ASHANTI YORUBA
    IVORY GOLD   IBO
    COAST COAST SLAVE CAMEROON
              COAST
                LOWER
                GUINEA   KIKUYU
                LUANGO   EAST
CARIBBEAN   CONGO   AFRICA ZANZI
SEA   KONGO   CENTRAL
                                   INTERIOR

Middle Passage

SOUTH AMERICA

ATLANTIC

OCEAN   ANGOLA

                NDONGO

                            MADAGAS

Tribes or nations labeled in **BLACK**.
Areas of slave trade labeled in RED.

20

States, primarily between the late 1600s and 1808, when the U.S. banned the importation of slaves from Africa. Captured Africans were transported in the holds of ships, such as that of the *Brookes* shown below, designed to utilize every inch for human cargo. Up to 20 percent did not survive the Atlantic crossing. In North America, the Africans might be sold individually at any ship dock, but most were sold at the major port cities of the Chesapeake Bay and, later, Charleston, Savannah, and New Orleans.

This early 20th-century photograph from the Belgian Congo of the internal African slave trade symbolizes the horrors and persistence of slavery—a counterpoint to the brass depiction of an African king.

Store Room

27 Store Room

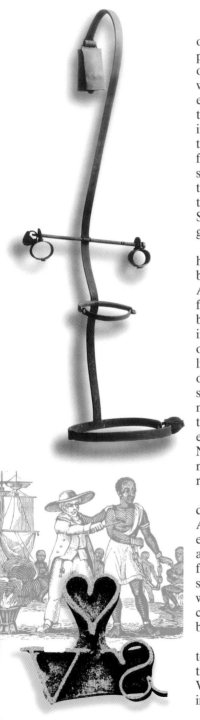

Slavery in the New World began simply as one part of a long history of international trade in goods and people both in Europe and in Africa. Slavery developed differently in different colonies, but the institution was recognizable. Many civilizations of the past had embraced forced labor and every continent, including the Americas and Africa, had witnessed it prior to the initiation of the transatlantic slave trade in the 16th century. Many blacks who arrived in the New World, therefore, were familiar with a system of labor known as slavery. In Africa, slavery had been practiced in Algiers, the Sudan, the Hausa city states, Zanzibar, and among the Fulani and other ethnic groups, including the Wolof, Sherbro and Mende, the Temme, Ashanti, Yoruba, Kongo, Lozi, and Duala.

Their familiarity with the institution in their ancestral homelands, however, did not diminish the horrors the blacks were to encounter in the Americas. Slavery in Africa usually was quite different from New World forms. In Africa slaves usually were persons who had been captured in war, although some were born or sold into bondage. Treatment often depended on the origin of their status. Prisoners of war generally had a harsher life. They could be sold and frequently were. Women often were forced into concubinage. Some were even sacrificed by victorious kings or rulers in religious ceremonies. Others were held for many years, sometimes through generations, and became part of the clan, or extended family, and were treated as valued workers. Native-born slaves, on the other hand, customarily were not sold and had some important privileges such as the right to inherit property and to marry free people.

Indigenous African slavery seemed to be more conducive to family stability and cohesiveness than the American institutions. Some West African societies, for example, forbade interference in a slave's marriage and allowed slaves to buy their freedom and the freedom of family members. Others forbade masters from having sexual relations with their slaves' wives. Some freed women when they gave birth. They also had greater class mobility with some passing from slave status to become soldiers and artisans.

Slavery in any society usually can be explained better, however, through a discussion of the slave's restrictions rather than his or her privileges. Most precolonial West African slaves could not become priests, hold important religious posts, or visit sacred places or the residence of the local chief. Some were not allowed to dress as free persons, or marry or be buried near them.

Slavery in Africa, as elsewhere, was not a static institution. It changed drastically over time usually as a response to cultural, economic, and military factors. The invasions of North African Arabs in the 11th and 12th centuries and the Europeans from the 16th through the 19th centuries caused great escalations in the numbers enslaved and tremendous changes in the status and function of the enslaved. The desire and, eventually, the need of West Africans to trade with Europeans for weapons and other prized goods prompted some Africans to get involved in the slave trade to such an extent that they could no longer draw on their traditional reserves of slaves.

The Atlantic slave trade was dangerous, controversial, and lucrative work. For Europeans in particular the trade was extremely profitable. It was indeed the foundation on which colonial agriculture and shipbuilding and European mercantilism and industry were built in the 17th and 18th centuries. The slave trade also brought profits to African middlemen, or caboceers, and the chiefs and rulers who traded their gold, ivory, dyewoods, slaves, and foodstuffs for European weaponry, textiles, liquor, glass beads, and brass rings. As greater demands from the New World made the trade more lucrative, more and more slaves were abducted through armed raids.

African villages, however, did not passively comply with slave trading raids; they fought back. Famed Ibo autobiographer Olaudah Equiano noted that the phenomenon of enemies coming into his village to take slaves was so prevalent during his childhood that often the men and the women took weapons to the fields in case of a surprise attack. "Even our women are warriors," Equiano recalled, "and march boldly out to fight along with the men. Our whole district is a kind of militia." Other West Africans who had been harassed by slave procurers went to the source of the problem, European traders, and attacked the company forts. Would-be slaves tried all kinds of ways to escape, sometimes sneaking away, getting help from people passing by, overpowering the guard watching them, and committing suicide. Most of them did not escape, but they did establish a tradition of resistance that followed the slaves to the Americas.

Once they reached the forts on the coast, slavers

Masters and overseers punished slaves for insubordination, not working hard enough, attempting to escape, inciting other slaves to rebel, and countless other infractions, such as dropping a glass of water. A Louisiana slave named Gordon, below, escaped to Union lines in 1863, and photographs of the welts and scars on his back publicized the horrors and violence of the slave system. Some slaves, especially those who tried to escape, were forced to wear bells, left, on their arms, neck, or head. Some were muzzled. Owners occasionally branded their slaves like cattle. The initials and a heart, left, are one example of a branding iron.

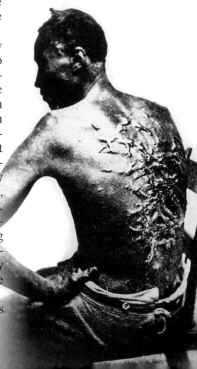

"The first object which saluted my eyes when I arrived on the coast was the sea, and a slave ship.... These filled me with astonishment, which was soon converted into terror." —*Olaudah Equiano*

placed them in temporary holding pens known as baracoons. The capture and transport to baracoons was a brutal experience physically and emotionally for the Africans. Their greatest anxiety derived from their fears—of their slavers, the slave ships, and their fate. Olaudah Equiano's response probably was a typical one. "The first object which saluted my eyes when I arrived on the coast was the sea, and a slave ship, which was as then riding at anchor and waiting for its cargo," Equiano recalled. "These filled me with astonishment, which was soon converted into terror." He had entered a completely different world. None of what he had experienced, however, from the time of his capture to his arrival on the coast in a slave coffle, had prepared Equiano for the horrors of the Middle Passage, the trip across the Atlantic Ocean.

Equiano did not know what to make of these strange people who looked, spoke, and behaved so differently from himself. "I was now persuaded that I had got into a world of bad spirits," he recalled, "and that they were going to kill me. Their complexions too differing so much from ours, their long hair, and the language they spoke, which was very different from any I had ever heard, united to confirm me in this belief....[Q]uite overpowered with horror and anguish, I...fainted."

Conditions aboard the slave ships during their voyages from Africa to America, which could take three weeks to three months, often were torture. Segregated by gender, the blacks were chained together and packed so tightly that they often were forced to lie on their sides in spoon fashion. Clearances in ships' holds often were only two to four feet high. During periods of good weather, the slavers allowed the Africans on deck for sun and washing. In bad weather or because of some perceived threat, they had to remain below, chained to one another, lying in their own feces, urine, blood, and vomit. "The floor of the rooms," one 18th-century ship observer wrote, "was so covered with blood and mucus which had proceeded from them in consequence of dysentery, that it resembled a slaughter house." Both shipboard personnel and American coastline observers reported that sometimes an approaching slave ship could be smelled before it could be seen.

Olaudah Equiano, left, was kidnapped from his Ibo tribe at age 11, enslaved in Africa, and passed from slave trader to trader. In his autobiography, below, first published in 1789, Equiano wrote of the "brutal cruelty" he saw aboard a slave ship and of his years in bondage as a seaman between Virginia, England, and Barbados. He eventually bought his freedom and became an abolitionist. Facing an uncertain future like Equiano, young boys huddle together in an illustration, lower left, from an 1857 issue of The Illustrated London News.

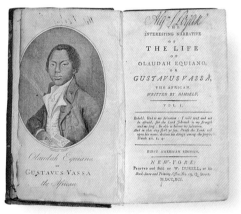

More than 200 attempts at on-board slave mutinies are documented. Slaves also resisted through hunger strikes, violent outbursts, refusal to cooperate, and suicide. Mortality rates varied greatly: sometimes as low as 10 percent, rarely as high as 100 percent. Still, it is estimated that several million Africans died before they ever reached the Americas.

The first blacks to arrive in the British colony of Virginia reportedly came in 1619. The previous summer the English ship *Treasurer* left Virginia to acquire salt, goats, and other provisions. Shortly thereafter, it came into contact with a Dutch man-of-war, and the two vessels sailed on together. They "happened upon" a Spanish frigate carrying slaves and other cargo. They seized the Spanish vessel and divided the cargo between them. Exactly how many Africans the Spanish ship was carrying we do not know, but the Dutch ship took on 100 and sailed back to Jamestown after becoming separated from the *Treasurer.* By the time it arrived in Jamestown in August 1619, there were 20 Africans aboard; the other 80 had died at sea. The *Treasurer* eventually reached Jamestown, too, with one African. The others—perhaps as many as 29—had been sold in Bermuda. From that point, Virginia's black population grew slowly but steadily; there were 300 blacks in 1649 and 2,000, or five percent of the population, by 1671.

The first Africans in Virginia, however, had an uncertain status. Slavery was not a formal, legalized institution in the colony until the 1660s, and subsequent laws made slavery more inescapable for more Africans as larger numbers of them began to arrive. The system's increasing presence can be attributed to numerous conditions. Most important, indentures did not keep pace with the growing needs for labor. Colonial administrators also actively encouraged black slavery, extending in 1635 the headright system, which rewarded those who imported persons to the colonies with 50 acres of Virginia land for each person so imported, to also include those who sponsored the arrival of blacks. At about the same time, there was a belief that blacks, unlike Europeans or the indigenous peoples, could work in the hot Southern sun and that they had a natural immunity to diseases like malaria and yellow fever. Moreover, the rise of the Company of Royal Adventurers Trading to Africa and its later merger with the Royal African Company guaranteed mainland planters greater access to slave imports. By the end of the 17th century, therefore, increasing numbers of slaves were entering Virginia and other colonies. Soon they were even the majority in many of Virginia's tidewater and Southside counties (those south of the James River). By 1750, they numbered more than 101,000 in Virginia while whites numbered 130,000.

By the 1670s, Africans lived in all of the British mainland colonies. Slaves were mentioned in Maryland's official documents by 1638, and the colony legally formalized the institution in 1663. The Lords Proprietors of Carolina, four of whom were members of the Royal African Company, expected slavery to play an important role in that colony's economic development and guaranteed its practice even before settlement. They, too, offered economic inducements for slave importation through the headright system. By 1710, the black population of 4,100 in what would become South Carolina almost equaled that of the whites. When the colony separated in 1729, South Carolina had 10,000 whites and 20,000 slaves while North Carolina had 30,000 whites and 6,000 slaves.

Georgia was late to embrace the institution. It legally banned slavery at the colony's founding, but, at the behest of settlers who saw slavery flourishing in neighboring South Carolina, Georgia repealed the prohibition in 1750. Advertisements in the colony's *Gazette* soon read like so many others of the era: "To be Sold on Thursday next, at publick vendue. Ten Likely Gold Coast New Negroes. Just imported from the West Indies, consisting of eight stout men and two women."

Blacks were slaves in the Dutch colony of New Netherlands long before the British took over the colony in 1664 and renamed it New York. Slaves from Angola and Brazil routinely worked the farms of the Hudson River Valley even though the British did not legalize the institution until 1684. By the end of the 17th century, only slightly more than 2,000 were in the colony, but by 1771 the 20,000 slaves made up nearly 12 percent of New York residents.

New Jersey under the Swedish and Dutch had few slaves, but that changed once the British gained control of the colony in 1664 and, as in South Carolina and Virginia, offered land incentives for the importation of Africans. By 1745, New Jersey had 4,600 slaves in a total population of about 61,000.

Bondage fell on less fertile ground in Pennsylvania, where Quakers, for moral reasons, and artisans, on eco-

Slaveholders constantly feared slave insurrections. To curb plots, Southern states passed laws intended to intellectually and physically isolate slaves and instituted practices that robbed them of their dignity. Despite dozens of conspiracies, few rebellions occurred. Three events that received widespread publicity were Gabriel's Conspiracy and Nat Turner's Revolt, both of which led to intensified restrictions, and the *Amistad* mutiny. In 1800, Gabriel and about 30 other blacks conspired to take hostages and public buildings in Richmond, Virginia, and to negotiate freedom for the slaves. The plot was betrayed before it was implemented. Testimony at the trials of the conspirators persuaded Virginians that insurrection was a daily possibility. But it was not until August 22, 1831, that Nat Turner, below, and five other slaves initiated a rebellion in Southampton County, Virginia. Turner's followers grew to about 60 as they traveled through the countryside killing at least 57 white men, women, and children. Over several days the conspirators, and many blacks not involved, were shot or captured. Turner eventually was caught and executed, as were 16 of his followers. Another insurrection involved the Spanish slave ship *Amistad*, right, which was off the coast of Cuba in June 1839 when 53 Africans freed themselves and, led by Joseph Cinque, far right, demanded that they be taken back to Africa. The crew, however, sailed the ship up the U.S. coast. The mutineers were captured by an American ship and put on trial in Connecticut. The court ruled that the Africans had

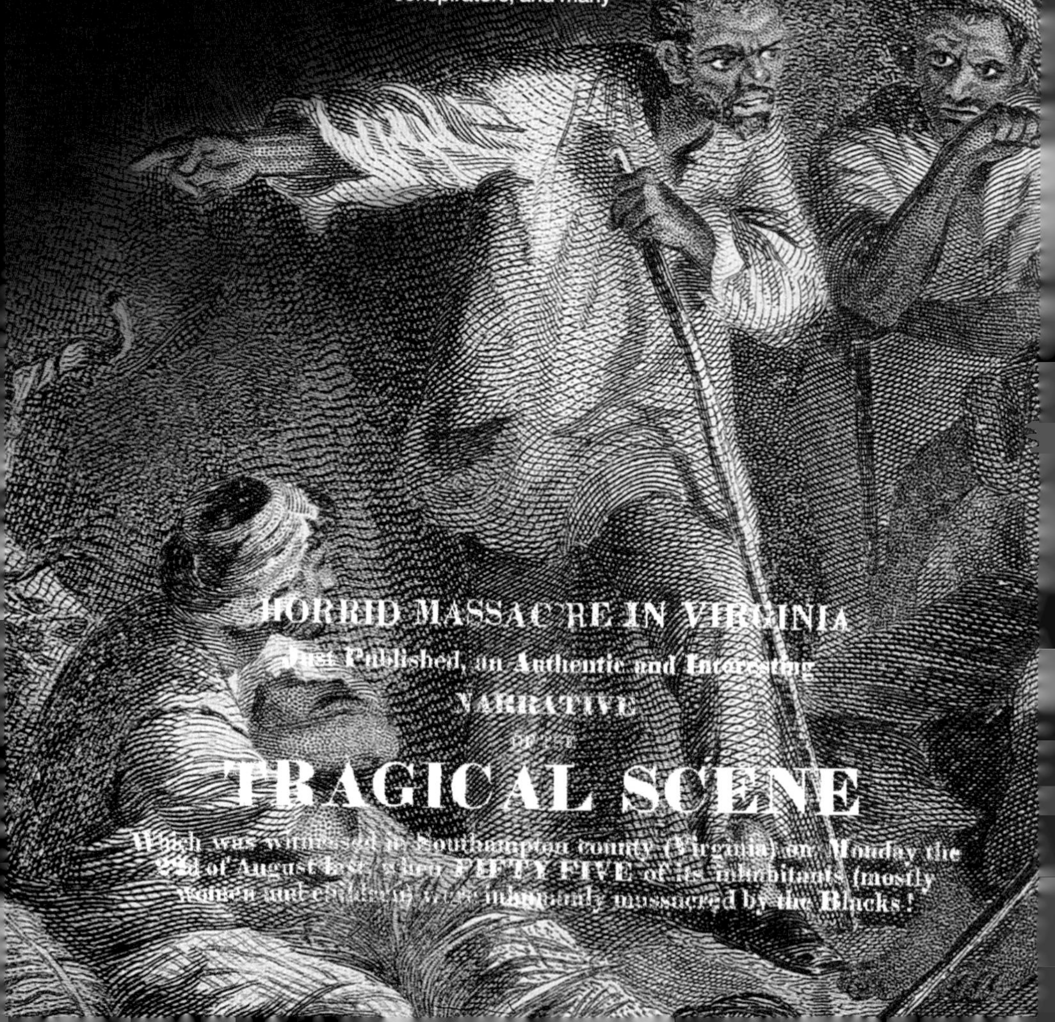

HORRID MASSACRE IN VIRGINIA

Just Published, an Authentic and Interesting

NARRATIVE

OF THE

TRAGICAL SCENE

Which was witnessed in Southampton county (Virginia) on Monday the 22d of August last, when FIFTY FIVE of its inhabitants (mostly women and children) were inhumanly massacred by the Blacks!

been illegally captured and sold and had a right to rebel, an opinion upheld by the United States Supreme Court.

nomic principle, opposed any increases in slavery. Before William Penn received his land grant, however, the Dutch had imported African slaves. And there always were those who wanted slave labor as eagerly as the Royal African Company wanted to sell slaves. The conflict was symbolized by the tax placed on slave imports by Pennsylvania: a duty of 20 shillings for every African imported in 1700 was doubled in 1705. When the colony's Assembly passed another law in 1712 that completely outlawed the importation of blacks, the Royal African Company persuaded the Privy Council in England to nullify the law. By 1750, Pennsylvania had approximately 11,000 slaves, most of whom were living in Philadelphia.

The New England colonies imported fewer slaves than the Middle or Southern colonies, but African slavery also was a part of their economy and culture. By 1715, there were approximately 2,000 slaves in Massachusetts and 1,500 in Connecticut. During the early 1770s, on the eve of the American Revolution, Rhode Island boasted a slave population of almost 3,800 while New Hampshire had only 654 slaves in a total population of about 62,000.

Unlike voluntary immigrants, Africans did not leave or arrive in family groups. They also had little opportunity to form family groups for several years after their arrival, because a typical cargo included twice as many males as females. Strangers in a foreign land, forced to comprehend a new language spoken by people who looked and behaved so differently from themselves, confronted with racism, sexism, hunger, epidemics, back-breaking work quotas, and harsh corporal punishment, these first few Africans spread thinly throughout the colonies undoubtedly suffered great emotional and physical distress. Slave owners conducted a general "seasoning" aimed at acclimating "outlandish" Africans so they might know their "place" and function appropriately in the system. Slave responses to this process varied tremendously. Even those Africans who lived with numerous other blacks might need anywhere from two years for minimal "seasoning" to four years for learning a functional creole language. For many, it took an entire lifetime or generations to reconcile their African cultural heritage and perspectives with their new lives as slaves in America.

Agricultural labor was not foreign to them. Slaves performed a number of diverse tasks from the very beginning of their presence on the North American mainland, but most were farm workers. Rising early in the morning to the sound of an overseer or driver blowing a horn and working until nightfall for five and one-half to six days a week, slaves planted, grew, harvested, and helped to ready crops for local, domestic, and international markets.

In colonial Virginia and North Carolina, they raised tobacco, corn, wheat, and other grains, grew vegetables, and raised livestock. South Carolina piedmont slaves produced tobacco, corn, and indigo. Those along the coastal plain of that colony and Georgia used their rice-growing skills they brought from their native African societies to reap great fortunes for their owners.

In the Northern and Middle colonies their labor was more diverse because of the shorter growing season. They mostly worked on small farms, dairy farms, and cattle-raising estates. They cultivated vegetables, tended livestock, and served as house slaves. Others worked in shipbuilding and mercantile enterprises and as artisans of one sort or another.

The development of black slavery as an institution and racism as an underlying ideology progressed with little public opposition or even debate until the era of the American Revolution. But this opposition, much of it disparate and disorganized, did yield results and did change the character of slavery by the end of the Revolutionary period. First, and perhaps most important, slavery had become a Southern phenomenon. Slavery was abolished or gradually eliminated through measures created in 1780 in Pennsylvania, in 1783 in Massachusetts, in 1784 in Connecticut and Rhode Island, in 1785 in New York, and in 1786 in New Jersey. In 1787, Congress prohibited slavery in the Northwest Territory. Scores of slaves were freed in the Upper South after the American Revolution, and the colonization of blacks in the Caribbean or West Africa was being entertained as a viable "solution" to the problem of free blacks in a society that embraced black slavery.

Slavery had changed with the American Revolution, but dependence on slave agricultural labor was growing rapidly in the Southern states. The profitable cultivation and ginning of short staple cotton made possible by the cotton gin in 1793, the expansion of U.S. territory in the Lower South and Southwest and West, and slave labor fueled an economic boom that lasted until the Civil War. It made an extremely small portion of South-

Slaves in Charleston, South Carolina, had to wear tags that identified their skill, such as carpenter or mechanic, and the year that the tag was issued. After 1848, free blacks in Charleston also had to wear tags declaring their status (see page 37).

31

Male and female slaves, including children, worked side by side in the fields raising and harvesting such crops as tobacco and cotton, as in this painting by Jerry Pinkney. Often one black male was singled out to be the driver, or leader, to make sure the crew carried out its tasks. He might be given certain privileges, such as a larger cabin and finer clothing than the others received. Some slaves, mostly women, worked in the master's house as cooks, maids, or, like the Louisiana black at upper left, nursemaids caring for the young white children. Although household slaves worked under better conditions than field hands, they constantly were under the watchful eyes of the master and mistress and had little privacy. Sometimes field hands were brought into the house or domestic workers were sent to the fields. All worked long, hard hours.

ern society extremely wealthy and powerful, perhaps more so than any other group in the young nation.

Cotton was king. National production of raw cotton, a major U.S. export to Europe, increased 921 percent, from 349,000 bales in 1819 to 3.2 million in 1855. This explosion in production led to an insatiable demand for slaves, particularly in the Deep South. Between 1820 and 1860, the number of slaves increased by 257 percent, to nearly four million. At the same time, the concentration of Southern blacks was shifting dramatically from the Upper to the Lower South. For instance, the slave population of the Lower South increased 34 percent from 1850 to 1860 while in the Upper South it rose only 9.7 percent.

The labor that slaves performed greatly influenced the quality of their lives. With few exceptions, men and women generally did the same kind of field work. The slave Austin Steward, for example, noted that on the plantation on which he worked "it was usual for men and women to work side by side...and in many kinds of work, the women were compelled to do as much as the men." Some males did perform more physically strenuous work, and few females held supervisory roles, such as driver, that males routinely occupied. Women, nonetheless, usually worked longer hours, spinning, weaving, nursing, and cooking for their owners once their field work was over, then doing all their own child care and domestic chores in the slave quarters.

Male slaves fared better materially than their female counterparts. When distributing food rations, slaveholders rarely gave females as much meat, meal, or other items as they gave males. Since slave women usually lived with their children and had to share some of their smaller portion with them, a mother's food allotment was especially sparse. Some fathers who lived away from their wives and children may have put aside part of their food allowance for their families, but owners did not compel them to do so. Similarly, the long pants, shirts, jackets, and other clothing that masters provided male slaves twice a year were much more appropriate for bending, stooping, and repelling insects endemic to field labor than the skirts and dresses females had to wear. Slave owners might have expected women to work as hard as men, but they were unwilling to provide women with equal material support.

While the vast majority of slaves worked in the fields, up to ten percent of them were occupied otherwise. In

Slaves, such as these shown in the 1860s on a South Carolina plantation, spent late evening hours and Sundays outside their quarters tending to their own domestic chores. They held religious meetings and dance parties often out of sight and hearing of whites. J. Antrobus's painting shows a burial service in Louisiana. Events like these strengthened a sense of community and helped to blend varied African traditions into an African-American culture. One symbol of that culture was the mbanza, below right, made out of a gourd and animal skin. By the 1800s, this African musical instrument had evolved into the American banjo played by both blacks and whites.

Some free persons were always among the Africans in North America. European ship crews included Africans who stayed on the continent, and some Africans brought to labor in North America used their skills or the uncertainty of laws to gain their freedom. Beginning in the 1640s, the legal net supporting lifetime indenture tightened and few Africans could claim a right to freedom by the end of the 1600s. In the 1700s, the slave population grew rapidly through importation and birth, but the free black population grew through natural increase, freeing by masters, self-purchase, and some successful escapes. Free blacks married both slaves and other free blacks, Native Americans, West Indians, and sometimes European servants. In 1770, Crispus Attucks, a longtime runaway, was killed by the British soldiers during the Boston Massacre. During the American Revolution, many African Americans fled to the British side or joined the patriot cause in search of freedom. Some who served in the Continental Army were freed, and the doctrines of liberty and human rights, so prominent in the rhetoric of the Revolution, caused the Northern states to abolish the slave trade and begin gradual emancipation while the Upper South made individual emancipations easier. In these regions, the number of free blacks doubled or tripled or more between the adoption of the U.S. Constitution in 1787 and the War of 1812. But the prosperity of Lower South slaveholders and the fear that free blacks would undermine the rationale for slavery terminated emancipations in the South. In the 1800s, free blacks increased in number through births and self-purchase. Northern free blacks tended to live in cities

where work opportunities were greater, while Southern free blacks were both rural and urban. By 1861, free-black communities could be found throughout the United States. The 1860 census revealed 3,953,760 slaves and 488,070 free blacks. The free blacks included, from left: Benjamin Banneker, who compiled six almanacs and helped survey the District of Columbia's boundaries in 1791; Isaac Jefferson of Monticello, who later moved to Ohio; Tom Molineaux, who gained his freedom by defeating other slaves at boxing; and an unknown woman.

MINNESOTA

WISCONSIN

MICHIGAN

IOWA

ILLINOIS   OHIO
         INDIANA

MISSOURI

KENTUCKY

TENNESSEE

ARKANSAS

MISSISSIPPI

ALABAMA

TEXAS

LOUISIANA

MAINE
abolished 1783

VERMONT   NEW HAMPSHIRE
abolished 1786   *abolished 1783*

NEW YORK   MASSACHUSETTS
gradual   *abolished 1783*
emancipation
1785   RHODE ISLAND
                   gradual emancipation
PENNSYLVANIA   *1784*
gradual   CONNECTICUT
emancipation   *gradual emancipation 1784*
1780
                   NEW JERSEY
                   gradual emancipation 1786

MARYLAND

DELAWARE

VIRGINIA

NORTH CAROLINA

SOUTH
CAROLINA

GEORGIA

FLORIDA

Slavery was permitted throughout the 13 original colonies. Between 1780 and 1786, some states (white labels) either abolished slavery or allowed for gradual emancipation. By 1860, only 15 (black labels) of the 33 states permitted slavery. It was not permitted in the Northwest Territory (Ohio, Indiana, Illinois, Michigan, Wisconsin, and a part of Minnesota). Slavery was also not allowed in California and Oregon. In the other territories the issue was left to local decision, a constant source of political tension and national division.

urban settings, females worked as waitresses, washer-women, midwives, domestics, and in factory maintenance. Male slaves had more access to skilled positions and exclusively held the more lucrative and prestigious jobs of blacksmith, cooper, painter, wheelwright, carpenter, tanner, joiner, cobbler, miner, and seaman.

Slaves began working at about age six or sometimes earlier if they seemed physically mature. Boys traditionally learned how to herd and tend livestock, pick up trash and stones, gather moss and other grasses, and carry water. Girls did similar tasks but also helped care for young children and worked in the kitchen. Both boys and girls picked fruit, nuts, and berries, pulled weeds and worms, and occasionally served as companions for their master's young children. Childhood was a time when slaves began to learn not only work routines but work discipline and related punishment.

Slaveholding women usually were in charge of disciplining slave children who worked in and around their master's home. One ex-slave interviewed in 1841 stated that whenever his mistress did not like his work she would hit him with tongs or a shovel, pull his hair, pinch his ears until they bled, or order him to sit in a corner and eat dry bread until he almost choked. George Jackson recalled that his mistress scolded and beat him when he was pulling weeds. "I pulled a cabbage stead of weed," he confessed. "She would jump me and beat me. I can remember cryin'. She told me she had to learn me to be careful...." These kinds of "lessons" hardly ceased as a slave matured.

Slaves young and old had to complete their assigned tasks satisfactorily to escape punishment. Such reprisals usually meant verbal abuse for small offenses, but owners, overseers, and drivers did not hesitate to impose severe floggings and public humiliation or even sell those who did not or would not complete tasks or were disrespectful to authority figures. "Beat women! Why sure he beat women," former slave Elizabeth Sparks exclaimed. "Beat women jes' lak men." Slaves were stripped of their clothing, faced against a tree or wall, tied down or made to hang from a beam, their legs roped together with a rail or board between them, and severely beaten. The beatings provided owners and overseers with a vehicle to both chastise and symbolically strip slaves of their personal pride and integrity while invoking terrifying images of the master's power.

For slaves, the worst punishment imaginable was to

be sold away from one's family and friends. This phenomenon was tied more to economic variables than the owner's need to punish or chastise "troublesome" slaves. Amanda Edmonds recalled the regret she felt when watching her family's slaves sold to pay off debts after her father's death. "I know servants are aggravating sometimes and [you] wish they were in Georgia," she confessed in her diary, "but when I see the poor...and sometimes faithful, ones torn away so, I cannot help feeling for them."

The dramatic shift in slave concentrations from the Upper to the Lower South and Southwest brought devastating consequences in the domestic lives of slaves. Hundreds of thousands lost husbands, wives, sons, daughters, other kin, and friends to this internal slave trade. Would-be slaveholders regularly attended public sales for slaves that usually were held in a town square, on the front steps of the local courthouse or sometimes at the slave trader's place of business.

Owners who wished to sell slaves usually brought them to town a few days before the auction and temporarily kept them in the county jail as a security precaution. Prospective buyers or their representatives went to the jail to examine slaves, who sat there miserably contemplating their fate and what might happen to family members and friends.

The despair was tremendous. One slave imprisoned in Bruin's jail in Alexandria, Virginia, wrote a desperate plea to her free black mother who worked as a laundress in New York City. "Aunt Sally and all of her children, and Aunt Hagar and all her children are sold, and grandmother is almost crazy," Emily Russell wrote in January 1850, and she, too, would be sold if her mother did not soon raise enough money to purchase her. "O mother! my dear mother! come now and see your distressed and heart-broken daughter once more. Mother! my dear mother! do not forsake me, for I feel desolate! Please to come now." The young woman eventually was sold to a long-distance slave trader for $1,200, but she died on the way to the "fancy girl" prostitution market in New Orleans.

Unfortunately, slave owners often benefitted from and thus were willing to instigate or ignore the tragedies that crippled a slave family's emotional and physical well-being. Even the sexual abuse of slave mothers and daughters often meant a financial gain for owners, who could claim as their property the children

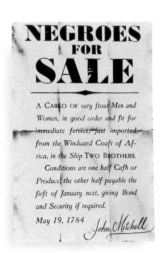

who might result since slave children derived their status from their mothers. Likewise, the domestic slave trade broke up families and extended kin networks. The loss of spouses and family members came to be so great in the Upper South that many children in the last slave generations grew up without the benefit of their mothers or fathers.

Despite the devastating impact of slave life on black kinship, the family was the slaves' most important survival tool. It flourished not so much because of its stability but its flexibility. The extended family of persons related by blood, marriage, and long-standing familial-like contact was its most persistent and essential characteristic. When fathers disappeared in the domestic slave trade, uncles and grandfathers often took on a paternal role for children left behind. Grandmothers and aunts nurtured, fed, and socialized motherless children. Young adults cared for the elderly whose children had been sold away. Extended kin did not replace husbands or wives lost forever to the Deep South but did offer some measure of comfort. Some slaves chose to remarry, and others were compelled by their owners to find another spouse to continue to have children who would become slaves.

Slave marriages were not recognized legally, but the weddings and commitments of African Americans were important events for slave families and communities. Georgianna Gibbs remembered that when the slaves on her farm married they had to "jump over a broom three times" before they actually were considered married. Some owners performed a brief service; others relied on slave or local ministers to officiate. A spirited celebration attended by family and friends usually followed with music, food, and dancing that often lasted most of the night.

Religion, dance, music, and food were vital aspects of the slaves' cultural life and exhibited traits drawn from their ancestral past in West Africa and their experiences in America. While many slaves converted to Christianity, especially as Baptists and Methodists, others held onto their Islamic faith and other religious rituals and beliefs derived from Africa. Like so much of slave culture, the religion in the quarters often was created from both sources. African traditions appeared in their musical instruments, medicines, and domestic wares, such as textiles, baskets, containers, and buttons. African slaves also helped introduce various West African foods like

millet, groundnut, benne, gourds, congo peas, and yams to America. Scholars have documented that the slaves' reliance on their own cultural references often allowed them to control aspects of their lives and withstand the psychological inhumanity of enslavement.

From the perspective of the slave, however, life was not experienced in this scholarly fashion. Slave life meant hard work, poor rations, sometimes brutal beatings, lost families, and illness. It also meant marriage on negotiated terms, but marriage nonetheless, and children who learned how to appreciate their kin, communities of friends, and, between hard times, laughter, pride, romance, song, dance, and God.

In a rare early photograph of slave life in the South, Timothy O'Sullivan's 1862 image shows five generations of one slave family on a Sea Island plantation near Beaufort, South Carolina, shortly after the Union army had liberated the island. Christian Mayr's 1838 painting depicts a slave wedding at White Sulphur Springs, Virginia, now West Virginia.

"I looked at my hands to see if I was
the same person now I was free.
There was such a glory over everthing,...
I felt like I was in heaven." —Harriet Tubman

Harriet Tubman (1823– 1913)
nurse, spy and scout

The Underground Railroad

By C. Peter Ripley

During the decades preceding the Civil War, when the United States struggled to define itself, no issue more divided and plagued its people than slavery. Even among those who had doubts about its morality, slavery was debated as part of a complex set of interlocking philosophical, social, economic, and political concerns too difficult to resolve and too intertwined with the fate of the nation to consider abolishing.

Yet in the midst of such moral confusion and political failure, black Americans, slave and free, aided by white allies, operated an illegal network determined to strike at slavery by helping those trapped in bondage. Hunted by the federal government, disapproved of by the Northern majority, and despised by the slaveholding South, the Underground Railroad served the nation as the exacting conscience of the most important reform movement in U.S. history—purging the land of slavery.

The Underground Railroad is one of American history's mysterious creations. It adopted such terms as "conductors," "stations," "routes," "cargoes," "packages," and "passengers" as suitable for its work even though it had no literal association with railroading; and "underground" was a fitting, and tantalizing, way to describe its activities, which were clandestine and illegal, best carried out away from the bright light of public examination. As a formal term, it refers to the movement of African-American slaves escaping out of the South and to the allies who assisted them in their search for freedom. Sharing nothing more than language and imagery with the steam technology of the day, the Underground Railroad is one of history's finest symbols of the struggle against oppression.

This movement of freedom-seeking slaves resists precise characterization even though it functioned from the founding of the Republic through the terrible bloodletting of the Civil War. It involved lone individuals and entire communities; defied conventions of race, class, culture, and gender; devised bold methods of escape; and was the scene of great human triumphs and

Harriet Tubman stands out as the icon of the Underground Railroad. The "Moses of her people" was born into slavery about 1820 in Dorchester County, Maryland. She was named Araminta Ross but was called Harriet by her owner. In danger of being sold away from her husband, John Tubman, and her extended family, she escaped alone in 1848 to Philadelphia. She returned to Maryland's Eastern Shore area about 20 times and led more than 300 runaways to freedom. During the Civil War, she returned to the United States from Saint Catharines, Canada, where she had settled, and served in the Union Army as a nurse, spy, and scout. Tubman died in 1913 at age 93.

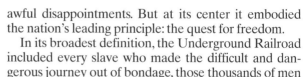

awful disappointments. But at its center it embodied the nation's leading principle: the quest for freedom.

In its broadest definition, the Underground Railroad included every slave who made the difficult and dangerous journey out of bondage, those thousands of men and women whose names are lost to history, and those fugitive slaves such as Frederick Douglass who became well-known leaders; countless other slaves who offered food, directions, and secrecy to runaways on the route to freedom; the occasional brave soul who made repeated trips into the South to guide slaves to the North, risking jail and perhaps death; and a secret network of fugitive slaves, free blacks, and whites of conscience who organized themselves to assist and protect the fleeing slaves. These blacks and whites served as "conductors" for their slave "passengers" and "cargoes" who were given sanctuary in the homes and farms and businesses that served as "stations" along the many escape "routes."

The experience of fugitive slaves William and Ellen Craft suggests the dramatic mix of individual initiative and organized assistance that often characterized the operation of the Underground Railroad. In December 1848, the Crafts waited at the Macon, Georgia, train station to board the Savannah-bound train. Both slaves, both illiterate, owned by different masters, the Crafts were poised to embark on a resourceful and daring escape to the North.

Ellen, the daughter of her master and one of his female slaves, was so light-skinned she posed as a frail, white slave owner. She carried her arm in a sling, covered her lower face with a poultice, hid her eyes behind dark green glasses, and wore a top hat to certify her assumed identity as a male. William played the role of the attentive slave accompanying the sickly master to Philadelphia in search of medical treatment. Traveling by train to Savannah, where they stopped overnight, then by steamer and another train to Baltimore, the Crafts experienced anxious moments among curious passengers and near discovery by railroad agents.

But on the Crafts' Baltimore train there also was a knowing free black passenger. Sensing that William might be a slave seeking freedom, the free black suggested that William contact a certain Quaker when he arrived in Philadelphia, and with that suggestion the guiding hand of the Underground Railroad touched the Crafts. Arriving at the Philadelphia train station,

Ellen clasped William's arm and said, "Thank God we are safe." The two exhausted fugitives then sought out that Philadelphia Quaker, who fed, housed, comforted, and kept them safe until it was time to conduct them to Boston, where the Crafts ended their 1,000-mile flight to freedom.

While the Crafts' story is documented as fact, the Underground Railroad is steeped in potent mythology, particularly the idea of a steady stream of brave conductors leaving a free state to make repeated trips into the South to guide slaves to freedom. That image is strong and the idea is grand, but such a dangerous operation was not the main work of the Underground Railroad except for such uncommon individuals as Harriet Tubman. After escaping from Maryland slavery in 1848, Tubman made nearly 20 trips into the South over the next decade to lead some 300 slaves to freedom. Tubman's heroic achievements earned her the respect and support of the Northern antislavery community and the fury of Maryland's planters, who so feared her they offered a $40,000 reward for her capture.

The actual starting date of the Underground Railroad could be fairly set when the first slave struck out for a free territory and the first person conspired to offer assistance. Perhaps it was a Georgia slave fleeing south to find protection among the Seminoles or in the Spanish settlements of Florida; or a Virginia slave who left the plantation aided by a local free black or other slaves who provided directions, food, a hiding place, and best wishes; or a post-Revolutionary War slave who crossed over the border from New York State into Canada as thousands of other blacks would do in the decades ahead.

As early as 1786 George Washington complained about trying to capture one of his fugitives from south-central Pennsylvania, "where it is not easy to apprehend them because there are a great number [of people there] who would rather facilitate their escape...than apprehend the runaway." The area along the Susquehanna River had attracted a number of former Virginia slaves who had gained their freedom by legal measures. Over the years, their numbers grew, and their community gained a reputation as a safe haven for slaves fleeing the South.

The rights of George Washington and his fellow slaveholders were recognized from the moment of the nation's creation by the U.S. Constitution, by federal

One of the most dramatic escapes was made by Ellen Craft, shown at left with and without her disguise, and her husband William, below. As they traveled from Georgia to Philadelphia, she posed as a white male seeking medical attention, and he played the loyal servant. The Crafts then moved on to Boston; they fled to England after the Fugitive Slave Law of 1850 was passed. The couple returned to Georgia after the Civil War and converted a plantation to a freedmen's school.

Routes to Freedom

Runaway slaves escaped to the North using a loose network of routes through the Southern border states. Those traveling in the East headed to such places as Philadelphia, New York, and Boston. Others fled into Ohio, Illinois, and Michigan. Some fugitives continued on to Canada, where slavery was outlawed and where officials refused U.S. requests for their return. Still others fled south to Florida and the Caribbean or into Texas and on to Mexico. Thomas Moran's 1862 painting, *Slave Hunt*, below, shows slaves fleeing through a swampy area. Most fugitives traveled on foot at night and hid by day in woods and swamps, along streams and rivers, or in homes and barns of free blacks and abolitionists. Some used small boats, hid in the backs of wagons, or stowed away on ships. Others devised unusual schemes. Henry Brown, right, had a shoemaker build a wooden box 2 feet wide, 3 feet long, and 2 feet 8 inches deep in which he had himself shipped by rail from Richmond, Virginia, to Philadelphia. He became known as "Box" Brown on the antislavery lecture circuit. In a less publicized but equally daring escape, Lear Green had herself shipped to Philadelphia in a sailor's chest. All fugitives could tell many stories about hiding from slave catchers as they moved from place to place not knowing what they might find for shelter and nourishment. But most did not publicize what they had done, so as not to endanger subsequent fugitives.

$150 REWARD.

RAN AWAY FROM THE SUBSCRIBER, ON THE NIGHT OF THE 27th OCTOBER,

A Negro Man named Ben,

Calling himself BEN. THOMAS.—On the day he absconded, by means of false keys, he open-

CANADA

UNITED STATES

MEXICO

Approximate route of flight

Free state

Slave state

Territories where slavery
permitted by local decision

One Fugitive's Story

James Lindsey Smith's story about his escape from slavery illustrates the trials and tribulations fugitives endured in their convoluted treks. On Sunday, May 6, 1838, Smith left **(1) Heathsville**, **Virginia**, at night with two others, Lorenzo and Zip. By canoe, they fled across the Coan River, took a small boat and sailed to just south of **(2) Frenchtown, Maryland**, where they started on foot toward New Castle, Delaware. Smith became exhausted, but Lorenzo and Zip pushed on because "our enemies are after us." After resting, Smith "took fresh courage and pressed… onward towards the north with anxious heart." Early Wednesday morning he heard a great rumbling. "I shook from head to foot as the monster came rushing on towards me." He escaped up an embankment from "the devil," a train. Trembling, hungry, and thinking "the patrollers were after me on horseback," he moved on and came upon a house where he asked a white woman for food. Invited in, he "ate up most everything she put on the table" and paid her 25 cents. He walked on to **(3) New Castle,** where he met up with Lorenzo and Zip. Astonished they had not been captured, they bought tickets and took a steamboat to **(4) Philadelphia**. Leaving Lorenzo and Zip, who were heading to Europe, Smith met a black man named Simpson, who secreted him in a little room after Smith finally admitted being a fugitive. Simpson met with some abolitionists, who decided to send Smith to Springfield, Massachusetts. On Friday, he left by steamboat for **(5) New York** with a letter to abolitionist David Ruggles. "I gave Ruggles the letter, and we had a great time rejoicing together." On Monday, with letters for a Mr. Foster in Hartford

and a Dr. Osgood in Springfield, Smith went to buy a steamboat ticket. He had been told the fare was $2, but the ticket clerk now said it was $3. "He "robbed me of every cent I had," $2.58. "I felt very much depressed….I was out of money and among strangers," but a waiter buoyed his spirits by giving him "an excellent supper." On Tuesday, he reached **(6) Hartford**, found Foster, who "raised three dollars for my benefit," and headed by steamboat to **(7) Springfield**.

He located Osgood, a Presbyterian minister, whose "family gathered around me to listen to my thrilling narrative of escape." Smith settled in the area, attended school, became a shoemaker and a preacher, married, and eventually settled in **(8) Norwich**, **Connecticut**. His full story appears in the book *Five Black Lives*.

and state laws, and by Southern custom and tradition, all of which made service or travel on the Underground Railroad dangerous and illegal. The Constitution guaranteed property rights, including ownership of slaves, each of whom the South was able to count as three-fifths of a person for the sake of representation in Congress. The Fugitive Slave Law of 1793 enforced those slaveholding rights and provided swift and simple procedures for slave owners or their agents to return into bondage any black person accused or even suspected of being a runaway slave. The accused possessed no right to an attorney or to a jury trial, and slave owners had but to state an oral claim of ownership to make their case before a magistrate. Anyone assisting or interfering with the arrest of a fugitive slave was subject to a $500 fine, Congress's way of acknowledging the existence and power of the Underground Railroad.

Southern state laws were even harsher, stipulating heavier fines and hard-labor jail time for anyone convicted of helping a slave on the run. And Southerners established rigid controls over slave behavior as a means of keeping them from freedom's trail. Plantation overseers, slave patrols, local law officials, and slave catchers whose job it was to track and capture runaways created a restrictive web that made illicit slave movement nearly impossible. So complete was the network that every white person had authority to stop any black person and demand to see either a slave's travel pass or a free black's emancipation papers. Without convincing documents, a black person could be taken to jail for further investigation. Southern whites tended to assume that any black person on the move was not on a legitimate errand.

Yet Southern slave communities devised brave and creative methods to skirt the pervasive controls that kept them in bondage. The Crafts' plan is certainly one of the best examples, but it has rivals, including the story of Henry Brown. A Richmond, Virginia, slave who worked in a city tobacco factory, Brown resolved to escape after his wife and three children were sold to a Methodist minister in North Carolina. Brown had himself sealed in a large wooden crate and shipped by Adam's Express to Philadelphia in 1848. After a 24-hour rail trip, Brown was met by members of the General Vigilance Committee of Philadelphia, the local Underground Railroad agency. Brown, as did the Crafts and many other fugitives, became a leading fig-

Sojourner Truth was an evangelistic orator who preached emancipation and women's suffrage. She was born a slave named Isabella Baumfree about 1797 in Hurley, New York. She first gained fame suing for the return of a son who had been illegally sold. Though she could neither read nor write, she was a compelling speaker at abolitionist meetings as she evoked the Bible and religious principles. She changed her name "because I was to declare truth unto people."

ure on the antislavery lecture circuit in the northern United States and in the British Isles. Brown's Richmond accomplice, Samuel A. Smith, a white shoemaker who had nailed shut the crate and shipped the fugitive, was found out and served seven years in prison.

But for the majority of runaways, courage and determination rather than dramatic creativity were their methods and means. Some stowed away on ships, riverboats, and trains, but most walked the South's roads at night and hid in caves, swamps, and woods during the day. They avoided any human contact for fear of betrayal, and, yes, they followed the legendary North Star. Many slaves made their way alone, too fearful to trust any stranger, black or white, slave or freeborn. But thousands of others were assisted by fellow slaves who offered hiding places, food, clothes, and safe directions. The Underground Railroad was a dangerous place of hunger, bad weather, illness, fear of discovery or betrayal, the threat of patrols, slave catchers, and "Negro dogs" trained to hunt down runaways. The surviving documentation about being a fugitive slave in the South tells harrowing stories, some of triumph and freedom, others of capture and punishment, including branding, whipping, sometimes even crippling and death. The runaway slave's decision to abandon family and the familiar to strike out for freedom was brave and reckless. Most slaves chose not to go, refusing to leave wives and children, husbands and parents, or fearing the consequences if they were caught.

For the Deep South slave starting out from Louisiana, Mississippi, Alabama, Florida, Georgia, or South Carolina the trek was long, which diminished the chances of success. The distance separating slavery and freedom was too great. But for those thousands of slaves who made their way to the Upper South, or escaped from there, the likelihood of finding freedom increased dramatically. Freedom was just across the line from Virginia, Maryland, Delaware, and Kentucky. In the Upper South, in the adjoining free states, and in the North's major cities, a more organized Underground Railroad network was active and attentive, ready to receive a passenger passed on by a fellow conductor and on the watch for telltale signs of an exhausted fugitive needing help.

History has kept as one of its mysteries the number of African Americans who made the journey. Estimates of the number of runaways range as high as 100,000

"The only true remedy for the extension of slavery, is the immediate abolition of slavery." —*Frederick Douglass*

PROSPECTUS
FOR AN ANTI-SLAVERY PAPER, TO BE ENTITLED
NORTH STAR.

FREDERICK DOUGLASS

Proposes to publish, in ROCHESTER, N. Y., a **WEEKLY ANTI-SLAVERY PAPER,** with the above title.

The object of the NORTH STAR will be to attack SLAVERY in all its forms and aspects; advocate UNIVERSAL EMANCIPATION; exalt the standard of PUBLIC MORALITY; promote the Moral and Intellectual Improvement of the COLORED PEOPLE; and hasten the day of FREEDOM to the Three Millions of our ENSLAVED FELLOW COUNTRYMEN.

The Paper will be printed upon a double medium sheet, at $2,00 per annum, if paid in advance, or $2,50, if payment be delayed over six months.

The names of Subscribers may be sent to the following named persons, and should be forwarded, as far as practicable, by the first of November, proximo.

FREDERICK DOUGLASS, Lynn, Mass.	JOEL P. DAVIS, Economy, Wayne County, Ind.
SAMUEL BROOKE, Salem, Ohio.	CHRISTIAN DONALDSON, Cincinnati, Ohio.
M. R. DELANY, Pittsburgh, Pa.	J. M. M'KIM, Philadelphia, Pa.
VALENTINE NICHOLSON, Harveysburgh, Warren Co. O.	AMARANCY PAINE, Providence, R. I.
Mr. WALCOTT, 21 Cornhill, Boston.	Mr. GAY, 142 Nassau Street, New York.

SUBSCRIBERS' NAMES.	RESIDENCE.	NO. OF COPIES.

prior to the Civil War. Many slaves who started out returned to their plantations, were captured, or otherwise failed to make it to free territory. Other estimates have 1,000 to 2,000 per year reaching freedom during the late antebellum years. Firm numbers require hard documentation, but most fugitive slaves were illiterate, left few records, and found few people interested in preserving their story.

In the Deep South, runaways relied upon free blacks and slaves willing to help fugitives they encountered. Escape routes and stations crisscrossed much of the Midwest and Northeast, although they shifted over time as danger of discovery or changes in leadership demanded. Two major routes extended from Kentucky and Virginia across Ohio to the North and from Maryland through Pennsylvania into New York or New England to Canada. There is substantial evidence of a long-running system of stations moving slaves through sparsely populated Illinois and Iowa into Canada.

This network of routes and stations grew out of a number of conditions—geography, personality, politics, religion, community values, and historical circumstances. Ohio developed one of the most impressive systems of stations in no small measure because of its location. It bordered Kentucky with more than 150 miles of river frontage and western Virginia with another 200 miles, making freedom only a river's width away for the Kentucky or Virginia slave or the Deep South slave who reached either state. The Ohio network evolved during the 1820s and 1830s when local blacks, many of them former slaves who had settled in Ohio towns and cities, began to conduct raids into Kentucky to liberate slaves and systematically aided others who came their way.

For 15 years John P. Parker was a conductor in the energetic riverboat town of Ripley, a main station in the Ohio network across from Kentucky. A former slave and an ironworker, he was among the few men in his community who, in his words, "made themselves poor serving the helpless fugitive." Parker's town was the setting of constant tension—a "real warfare" he described it—between those who sought to rescue slaves and those who patrolled nightly in hopes of catching fugitives for the reward offered by their masters. In most instances, Parker and his network assisted runaways who had made the river crossing by themselves, but during many suspense-filled nights, Parker belted on

UNDERGROUND RAIL ROAD

A RECORD

OF

FACTS, AUTHENTIC NARRATIVES, LETTERS, &C.,

Narrating the Hardships Hair-breadth Escapes and Death Struggles

OF THE

Slaves in their efforts for Freedom

...olition Society and
...nia Abolition Society
...med in the 1780s to
...slavery gradually
... legislative action and
... manumission. William
...arrison was a gradual-
...black friends soon
...led him to advocate im-
... and uncompensated
...bation in his newspa-
... *Liberator*. Immedi-
...ecame the new goal
...tionism. The New Eng-
...ti-Slavery Society was

...allies, including three blacks,
then formed the American Anti-
Slavery Society, which had
associate interracial female
societies in Philadelphia and
Boston. By 1838, this group
had almost 250,000 members.
The Society split into factions
at its 1840 convention in
Syracuse, New York, when a
woman was elected to a committee. Garrison's group became increasingly radical and
considered dissolving the
Union as the only way to force

...zed into the American and
Foreign Anti-Slavery Society
from 1840 to the mid-1850s
Gerrit Smith's political abolitionists in New York argued
that the U.S. Constitution prohibited slavery and that the
Federal Government had the
power to abolish it. Most poli-
cal abolitionists joined the n
Republican Party in 1854.
Some abolitionists, such as
Oberlin, Ohio, group shown
below, rescued slaves who
were about to be returned to

their masters. Black abolitionists often felt they were kept on the margins of the movement and increasingly had their own meetings and read newspapers published by African Americans. Abolitionism, despite its fragmentation, helped bring the nation to civil war.

Attending an 1845 antislavery meeting in Cazenovia, New York, are Frederick Douglass, to his left Theodosia Gilbert, and behind him Gerrit Smith.

Our Country is the World, our Countrymen are all Mankind.

BOSTON, FRIDAY, OCTOBER 23, 1857.

ANTI-SLAVE-CATCHERS'
MASS
CONVENTION!

All the People of this State, who are opposed to being made SLAVES or SLAVE-CATCHERS, and to having the Free Soil of Wisconsin made the hunting-ground for Human Kidnappers, and all who are willing to unite in a

In disputes over slavery in the Kansas territory in the 1850s, John Brown gained a reputation as an ardent abolitionist and believer in violence to pursue goals. He is best known for his October 16, 1859, raid on the federal armory and arsenal at Harpers Ferry. Brown's followers, included five free blacks, among them Dangerfield Newby from Virginia and Osborne Anderson from Chatham, Canada West. They hoped to seize a supply of weapons and spark a rebellion of the slaves. But federal troops under Col. Robert E. Lee stormed the enginehouse, right, and captured Brown and most of the raiders. He was found guilty of treason against Virginia and hanged December 2. Southern whites saw Brown as a violent fanatic. Northern abolitionists hailed him as a martyr. In a few years Union troops were singing "John Brown's body lies a-moldering in the grave, but his soul goes marching on." The song originally referred to another John Brown but later became associated with the abolitionist.

two pistols and a knife, took his boat into Kentucky, and brought out fugitives who were stranded just short of freedom's territory. Parker reported that he assisted 315 slaves during the first five years he was involved in the Ohio Underground Railroad.

During the 1830s and continuing late into the next decade, Washington, D.C., operated one of the most aggressive networks because of its location and its artful leadership. Thousands of slaves from plantations in bordering Virginia and Maryland were helped to freedom by Washington blacks, many of whom masked their illegal activities behind trusted positions in white society. They included ministers, businessmen, and a porter in the U.S. Supreme Court. Thomas Tilly, a coachman for a federal marshal, held religious services for slaves on neighboring Virginia plantations and used those occasions to organize escapes. Jacob R. Gibbs, a printer, maintained a file of "free papers" from deceased local blacks, which he gave to runaways to ensure their safe passage through white society. He aided as many as 2,000 fugitives.

Leonard A. Grimes, who worked as a cabdriver, used carriages and horses in his efforts. During one trip into Virginia, Grimes was captured liberating a slave woman and her seven children, a crime for which he served two years in a Richmond prison, only to rejoin the underground after his release. On one occasion, members of the Washington network rescued several fugitive slaves who had been captured and placed in slave pens until their masters could claim them. This eastern network was briefly crippled during the late 1840s by urban race riots and by slaveholders' attempts to crush the network that forced important members of the Washington group to flee the area.

Individual personalities shaped the character of some sections of the underground. Among the thousands of free-state agents were community leaders and work-a-day citizens—black and white, slave and free-born, men and women—committed to striking a blow at slavery. Fugitives who made their way from Philadelphia into Canada via the Albany, New York, route sometimes found themselves under the protective care of luminary black abolitionists and longtime agents: William Still in Philadelphia, David Ruggles in New York City, Stephen Meyers in Albany, J.W. Loguen in Syracuse, Frederick Douglass in Rochester, and Hiram Wilson in Saint Catharines, Upper Canada. Some mornings Douglass arrived at his Rochester newspaper office to find fugitives on the doorstep. The runaways were routinely hidden, fed, clothed, allowed to rest, and cared for in the home of a local agent before moving on to the next station, sometimes by foot, sometimes by train, sometimes hidden in a wagon traveling by night. Appropriately enough, Douglass's antislavery newspaper was named the *North Star*.

Some Underground Railroad stations possessed such forceful membership and moral authority that the network became a defining characteristic of the community. Those stations usually resulted from a number of influences coming together, including a sizable fugitive slave and free black population and an active Quaker fellowship, or some mix of race, church membership, family ties, and a strongly-held sense of the injustice of slavery. Oberlin, Ohio, was one such community, its reputation further enhanced by the robust abolitionist tradition of Oberlin College.

In one instance, slave catchers accompanied by a U.S. deputy marshal arrived in Oberlin to capture fugitive slave John Price. When residents learned of the plan, the Underground Railroad went on alert. Almost 40 local residents formed a rescue party—father and son, carpenter and farmer, cabinetmaker and cobbler, undertaker and brickmaker, student and professor, grocer and lawyer, black and white—sped to a nearby town and rescued Price from his captors. Thirty-seven were indicted for their roles in the rescue, twenty spent time in jail awaiting trial, and two were tried and convicted. Yet this experience failed to cripple the Oberlin network.

The best organized and most aggressive stations operated in Northern cities. These major hubs developed into a tight network that passed fugitives from city to city. Often known as vigilance committees, they were well-led, well-staffed, well-funded, and served as the runaways' friend and the conscience of the black community. They evolved during the 1830s out of cruel circumstances. As unprecedented numbers of fugitives began to settle in Northern cities, the kidnapping of fugitive slaves and free blacks by slave catchers, who sold their prey into slavery, became commonplace. The black community organized to protect itself and fleeing slaves.

The New York Committee of Vigilance, founded in 1835 and led by David Ruggles, relentlessly aided and

defended escaped slaves. White abolitionists provided important assistance, but blacks directed the committee and raised most of its operating funds. The New York station disseminated information about kidnappers and slave catchers; dispensed food, clothing, money, medicine, legal services, and temporary shelter to fugitives; and resettled them in the North or provided safe passage to Canada. It compiled the *Slaveholders Directory* to make public the names and addresses of police, judges, and other New York City officials who cooperated with kidnapping rings or aided in the capture of fugitives. The committee kept a particularly close watch on the city's harbor facilities, where Ruggles and his companions more than once risked their lives by boarding ships they suspected were concealing kidnapped victims or illegally transporting slaves into the United States.

Blacks—many of them fugitive slaves—also organized vigilance associations in Philadelphia, Boston, Detroit, and other Northern cities. Philadelphia, a city with large Quaker and black populations, was home to perhaps the most active Underground Railroad station. It directed some 9,000 runaways between 1830 and 1860 to contacts along well-established and well-maintained routes. William Still, a freeborn black, was one of its legendary leaders. As a member of the Pennsylvania Anti-Slavery Society and then as director of the General Vigilance Committee of Philadelphia, he managed the committee's finances, which funded Harriet Tubman's raids. He established a network of safe houses, maintained contacts along routes from the Upper South to Canada, and channeled runaways to conductors in Pennsylvania and New York.

Fugitive slaves, black sailors, stevedores, teamsters, and other black workers served as the muscle and backbone of the committee by sheltering and transporting fugitives and by gathering and relaying crucial information. One Underground Railroad member described them as "men of overalls...who could do heavy work in the hour of difficulty."

Vigilance committee membership brought working-class blacks into closer contact with more elite black abolitionists, who provided money and organizational experience. Black women kept a watchful eye out for suspicious whites they observed in hotels, in boarding-houses, and on the streets. Black congregations sheltered fugitives and opened their buildings to committee

Quakers Levi and Catherine Coffin welcome runaway slaves arriving at their home outside Cincinnati (where they had moved in 1846) in this detail from Charles T. Webber's influential painting, The Underground Railroad. *The Coffins had moved to Indiana in 1826 from North Carolina, where several members of the Coffin family were involved in helping fugitive slaves. In Indiana, they took in many groups of 2 to 17 fugitives and assisted them on their way northward. Levi Coffin, among others, became known as "president" of the Underground Railroad. Harriet Beecher Stowe based her fictional characters Simeon and Rachel Halliday in* Uncle Tom's Cabin *on Levi and Catherine Coffin.*

meetings; church-affiliated auxiliaries, often directed by black women, raised the bulk of committee operating funds; and black benevolent societies collected food and clothing for destitute fugitives. Hundreds of New York City blacks attended the committee's public meetings to listen to activity reports and to celebrate dramatic stories of fugitive slaves who had made successful escapes.

The Underground Railroad can be considered the most aggressive arm of the antislavery movement, but efforts to free slaves had been going on for quite some time. Slavery was gradually abolished in the Northern states in the wake of the American Revolution. Early in the 19th century, a movement began to organize to end slavery in the South, where slave labor was more intimately tied to the economy, more Africans were held in bondage, and the white population was more defensive about preserving the institution.

The abolitionist movement spread slowly until the 1830s, when its tone and tactics changed. In 1833 black and white abolitionists from nine states came together in Philadelphia to form the American Anti-Slavery Society, an organization designed to coordinate and promote local antislavery activity in the free states. From that point on, the abolitionist movement became more aggressive in its language and tactics, demanding the immediate end to slavery without compensating slaveholders for their losses. Other organizations were formed, and relying on the power of persuasion, newspapers were established and lecture tours were organized to spread the word throughout the North about the evils of slavery and the need for its eradication. Never winning over more than a small minority of Northern whites, the antislavery movement inspired the national debate over slavery, pushed the slaveholding South into a rigid defensive position, and helped prepare Northern sentiment to eventually accept abolition as an aim of the Civil War.

Not all abolitionists approved of the Underground Railroad, although antislavery organizations often funded its activities and in more than one community when the local antislavery organization ended its meeting, many members remained behind to convene a meeting of the vigilance committee. Service in the underground network was a dangerous trade requiring secrecy and determination and sometimes extracting enormous sacrifice. Black and white abolitionist news-

CAUTION!!
COLORED PEOPLE
OF BOSTON, ONE & ALL,

You are hereby respectfully CAUTIONED and advised, to avoid conversing with the

Watchmen and Police Officers
of Boston,

For since the recent ORDER OF THE MAYOR & ALDERMEN, they are empowered to act as

KIDNAPPERS
AND
Slave Catchers,

And they have already been actually employed in KIDNAPPING, CATCHING, AND KEEPING SLAVES. Therefore, if you value your LIBERTY, and the *Welfare of the Fugitives* among you, *Shun* them in every possible manner, as so many *HOUNDS* on the track of the most unfortunate of your race.

Keep a Sharp Look Out for KIDNAPPERS, and have TOP EYE open.

papers cautioned fugitive slaves not to discuss their escapes in detail to avoid having their routes shut off to those still in bondage. Messages passed between agents were filled with cryptic terms and vague references, a style that adopted railroading language familiar to the conductors but of limited use to strangers or enemies. Caution and secrecy notwithstanding, dozens of agents were jailed for aiding escaping slaves.

The antislavery movement wrote and spoke of Calvin Fairbanks, Charles Turner Torrey, and Jonathan Walker as martyrs, three chosen from among the many. Fairbanks was jailed twice, suffering 16 years of foul conditions in a Kentucky prison for aiding a slave family escaping to Canada. Charles Torrey, the conductor of perhaps 400 slaves before he was arrested, died of tuberculosis in a Baltimore prison. Jonathan Walker, a Massachusetts sea captain who hid four fugitive slaves aboard his ship had "S.S."—for "slave stealer"—branded on his right hand, served eight months in jail, and was forced to compensate the slaveholders for damages. The list goes on, white and black, slave and free, lingering in jails in both North and South.

More than one Underground Railroad agent was arrested attempting to rescue slaves who had been captured in the North and jailed to be sent back into slavery. The number of jailed fugitives and rescue attempts increased dramatically after Congress passed the Fugitive Slave Law of 1850, a point of departure in the history of the Underground Railroad. Prior to that date, underground agents and their fellow abolitionists were regarded as dangerous extremists by most Americans, even those who considered themselves freedom-loving. But the Fugitive Slave Law changed popular attitudes among many Northerners who viewed some provisions of the 1850 law as serious violations of cherished personal liberties and constitutional guarantees.

Underground Railroad activity and sectional tensions over slavery increased after 1850. More whites than ever before joined the predominately black network, more funds became available, new stations and routes were established, and influential lawyers offered their services to defend captured fugitives and agents arrested for aiding them. The need was considerable.

Blacks in the Civil War

The Civil War began as a war to preserve the Union, a nation Abraham Lincoln termed "half slave, half free." But no sooner had Union troops appeared in the border states, on islands off the Atlantic coast, and in the lower Mississippi Valley than thousands of blacks took the opportunity to liberate themselves by fleeing to Union camps. A first impulse to send them back to their masters was soon squelched. Runaways, such as those shown below on the U.S.S. *Vermont*, became "contraband," or confiscated property of war. Many of them quickly found work within the Union lines, and family members joined them. In the Confederate states, free blacks were conscripted to dig fortifications and to labor on roads and in mines. Slaves accompanied their masters to army camps as cooks, grooms, and personal attendants. Slaveholders hired out their slaves to the army, but as the Union army approached, many preferred to send their slaves to the interior lines. These enormous upheavals in Southern life created new opportunities for self-liberation. Meanwhile, Northern blacks who first sought to form military units and join the Federal army were rebuffed. Then in July 1862, after the disastrous Peninsular Campaign, President Abraham Lincoln issued the Second Confiscation Act stating that the Union could "employ...persons of African descent...for the suppression of the rebellion." The entry into the Union army of African-American

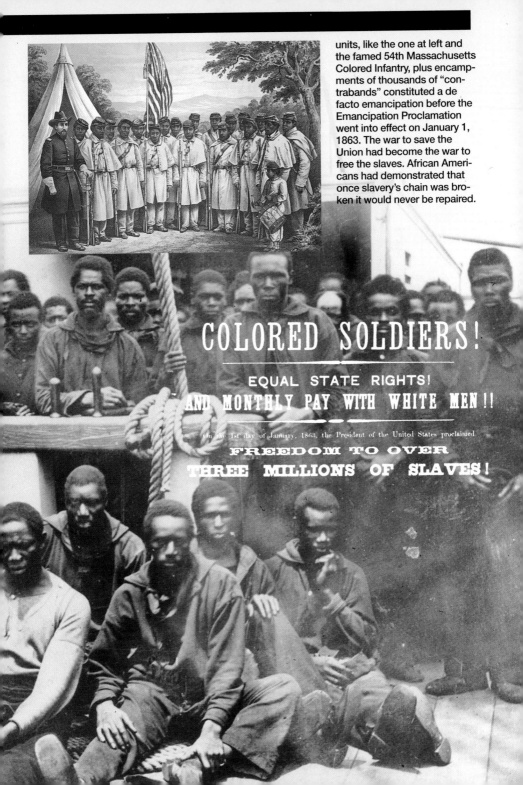

units, like the one at left and the famed 54th Massachusetts Colored Infantry, plus encampments of thousands of "contrabands" constituted a de facto emancipation before the Emancipation Proclamation went into effect on January 1, 1863. The war to save the Union had become the war to free the slaves. African Americans had demonstrated that once slavery's chain was broken it would never be repaired.

COLORED SOLDIERS!

EQUAL STATE RIGHTS!
AND MONTHLY PAY WITH WHITE MEN!!

On the 1st day of January, 1863, the President of the United States proclaimed

FREEDOM TO OVER
THREE MILLIONS OF SLAVES!

Growing bold because of expanded powers granted by the new federal law, slave catchers and kidnappers swarmed north threatening all blacks, not just fugitive slaves, with arbitrary arrest and a swift hearing before a federal officer followed by life in bondage. So real was the threat and so fearful the consequences, a startling number of blacks, many of them freeborn, fled the United States during the 1850s. In Michigan hundreds of blacks crossed the river from Detroit into Canada during the first months after passage of the law.

In nearly every major Northern city during the 1850s, rescuers of captured fugitives often resorted to violence, which had been considered by only a radical few during the years before the Fugitive Slave Law. Wherever the underground was active, blacks pledged their will "to resist to the death," as one handbill announced their intention. Rescues—failed and successful—were plentiful throughout the free states, some of them well organized, others spontaneous. One of the most celebrated rescues took place in Syracuse, New York, where black and white members of the local vigilance committee stormed the jail to free the fugitive slave Jerry McHenry and spirited him away to Canada. Federal prosecutors, eager to make an example of those who flouted the law and encouraged by President Millard Fillmore, indicted 26 men, including 12 blacks. Nine of the accused blacks, with leading black abolitionists Samuel R. Ward and Jermain W. Loguen among them, fled to Canada. Three whites were tried and acquitted. Enoch Reed, the single black tried, was convicted and jailed.

Fugitive slaves on the run sought a sanctuary, a place to stop, where they could make a new life free of fear. For some, that meant the towns and cities of the eastern free states. Others settled in the villages and farm lands of the Midwest, and many made their way to California, where more than one family lost track of fathers, brothers, and sons in the goldfields of the late 1840s. Fugitives who lacked confidence in America's legal and social values turned their attention to foreign points—to Canada for the majority, to the Caribbean or Latin America for the few.

Runaway slaves settling along the eastern seaboard found comfort and safety among the growing numbers of blacks who developed separate and vibrant communities in America's emerging urban centers. Boston, Philadelphia, and New York were conspicuous locations but not exclusively so. New Bedford, Massachusetts, one of many smaller examples, attracted a fugitive population because of its fishing and sailing trades.

Wherever they settled, former slaves were typically drawn into community life. Sharing the aspirations common to American culture, they found jobs, raised families, and assumed the responsibilities of citizenship. But citizenship and community building were difficult for African Americans during the antebellum years. Blacks struggled against racism, race violence, and an indifferent and hostile political and legal system that in its normal application afforded them little protection and few resources.

Self-reliance became the watchword. Blacks, free-born and former slave, built their institutions apart from the white majority. They founded and supported their own newspapers, *Freedom's Journal*, the *North Star, The Colored American, The Anglo-African,* papers dedicated to serving black needs, national and local, while joining the battle against slavery. *The Colored American* asked its readers "to speak out in Thunder Tones." Blacks built and funded their own churches, schools, and orphanages to nurture and serve community needs. They set up reading rooms to promote literacy, established lecture series to spread the good word, and in the spirit of the era of reform, they banded together in temperance and antislavery groups to change themselves and transform the nation.

Black institutions and organizations fostered racial pride and identity while becoming centerpieces for black activism and leadership. Veterans of the Underground Railroad were conspicuous participants. Frederick Douglass was at his editor's desk, and countless fugitives slaves stood behind the pulpit of their churches every Sunday morning preaching to their congregations about salvation and slavery. They included such well-established leaders as J.W.C. Pennington, Henry Highland Garnet, Jermain W. Loguen, and Samuel Ringgold Ward.

Churches and schools doubled as antislavery meetinghouses, naturally attracting former slaves, many of them not long off the Underground Railroad. Believing that Northern public opinion was the key to a successful battle against slavery, abolitionists published newspapers, books, and pamphlets, and they organized extensive lecture tours. The leadership learned very quickly that fugitive slave speakers had the greatest

Samuel Ringgold Ward was a Congregational minister and a stirring orator known as the "Black Daniel Webster." As an infant, he escaped slavery with his parents. As an adult he became a staunch abolitionist. He went to Toronto and founded a black newspaper, The Provincial Freeman. *Ward aided fugitives in Canada and traveled extensively in Britain advocating racial equality and raising funds for black causes.*

impact on audiences; someone "who has felt in his own person the evils of Slavery, and with a strong voice of experience can tell of its horrors," wrote one enthusiastic organizer of the lectures.

Fugitives took their story wherever they might be heard, to the cities and small towns across the North and Midwest, in meetinghouses and outdoor forums. They rode trains and dusty stagecoaches to address audiences that were sometimes hostile, even violent; Douglass had his wrist broken at an outdoor meeting in Indiana. They told personal tales of suffering and drama—the Crafts and Henry "Box" Brown were favorites—and they displayed slavery's tools—whips, branding irons, leg chains, and neck collars—to persuade an audience of slavery's inhumanity. And they were good at it, becoming the antislavery crusade's undisputed true voice and the cornerstone of its credibility.

Fugitives quickly learned what Northern free blacks always understood, that racism thrived in the North, that there was an intimate connection between racist behavior in the free states and bondage in the South, and to rid the land of one such evil and not the other would be to leave the job half done. So they organized campaigns to win the vote, to desegregate streetcars, and to see that a fair portion of local taxes supported their institutions. During those difficult days, in those troubled settings, former slaves shared the responsibility for creating black institutions and helped establish the leadership tradition of the black community.

Struggle as they might to make a life in the country they had helped build, many fugitive slaves grew discouraged. The courts denied them protection, the electoral system offered them no ballot, daily life was never far removed from reminders of segregation and discrimination, and the threat of race violence always churned on the surface of society. Little wonder that many fugitives chose to flee the country.

The overwhelming majority headed for Canada, at least 20,000 by the end of the Civil War, perhaps many more depending upon whose sketchy and incomplete numbers one accepts. But flee they did, out of harm's way into the welcoming embrace of the British empire that in the 1830s abolished slavery and then handed down legal decisions that protected fugitive slaves from being extradited back to the United States and back into slavery. Lewis Richardson, one of Henry Clay's

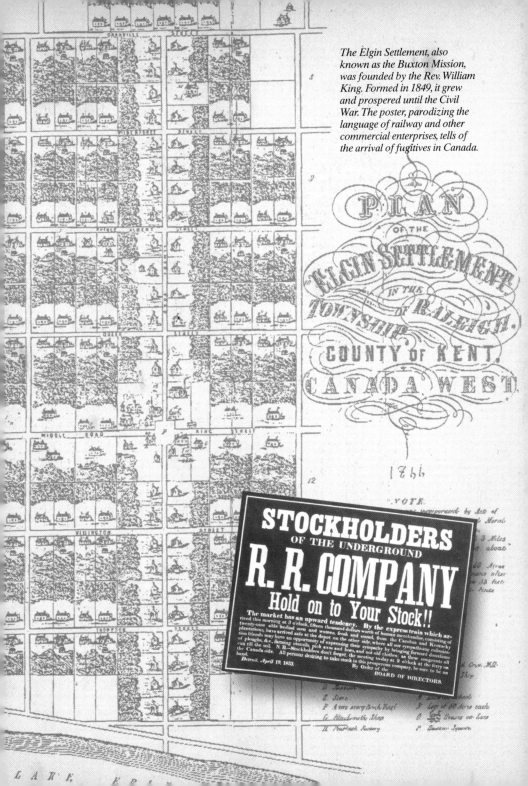

The Elgin Settlement, also known as the Buxton Mission, was founded by the Rev. William King. Formed in 1849, it grew and prospered until the Civil War. The poster, parodizing the language of railway and other commercial enterprises, tells of the arrival of fugitives in Canada.

former slaves, wrote of his relief at being on British soil, "where I am not known by the color of my skin, but where the government knows me as a man."

Canada was an appropriate final stop on the Underground Railroad, a safe haven that blacks discovered over time was not wholly free of racial problems but one that offered them a fair opportunity to do well and to make a life, and many former slaves did just that. They built houses, started businesses, and worked farms; they discovered fair treatment in the courts and open access to the voting booth; they formed social organizations and joined militia units; and they founded and published two newspapers, the *Provincial Freeman* and the *Voice of the Fugitive*. Nearly every center of black population had an organization devoted to keeping a watchful eye out for slave catchers who crossed the border trying to kidnap fugitives so they might return them to their masters—for a price.

The Canadian migration began as a hopeful terminus for the Underground Railroad, a remedy from slavery's extended grasp throughout the United States, particularly after 1850 and passage of the Fugitive Slave Law. But it became something more: a symbol of black determination and antislavery prophesy. Abolitionists in the United States argued that the slave's decision to make the dangerous trek on the Underground Railroad undercut the slaveowner's argument that Africans were contented in their life of bondage. And, continued the argument, once in Canada, blacks who thrived in a free and open society would effectively challenge proslavery claims of racial inferiority, claims that blacks were incapable of functioning on their own as emancipated citizens and therefore best left in bondage.

And nowhere was this symbolism more potently advertised and promoted than in two of the planned communities—Dawn and Elgin—that were established in Canada. Organized and funded by abolitionists and philanthropic groups and individuals, they were set up to assist fugitives, many of whom arrived with little more than a set of clothes and their exhaustion.

The Dawn and Elgin settlements were organized in the 1840s. Dawn attracted some 500 settlers to its 1,500 acres situated near Dresden. Its chief attraction, aside from the assistance and comfort of a shared community, was a manual labor school—the beloved promise of education. Near Buxton, Elgin became the most successful of the planned communities by 1861 with three schools, two hotels, a general store, and a post office to service the 300 families who resided on 9,000 acres. These communities were home to fugitive slaves, but they also took on great importance in the U.S. struggle over slavery. Guided by religion and education and dedicated to self-help and improvement, the settlements were promoted by abolitionists as proof of black fitness for freedom. The rationale was that if former slaves could make Dawn and Elgin showcases of black aspirations and achievement, their very example would undercut racist theories that Southerners and their friends used to defend slavery.

The communities never became what their organizers and antislavery promoters hoped for after their initial philanthropic impulse to assist escaping slaves was diverted to antislavery propaganda. Dawn shut down in the 1850s; Elgin struggled along for another 20 years. But these experiments do not stand alone in history. None of the reform-minded planned communities in North America prospered and flourished over the long haul, not those devoted to fugitive slaves or the ones idealistic whites established to illustrate the benefits of communal living. And life on the Canadian frontier was harsh even for the experienced pioneer. Towns and settlements sprang up and disappeared with alarming regularity regardless of race, origin, or ambition. The fate of Dawn, Elgin, or the others like them in Canada does little to diminish the life that thousands of blacks made for themselves in the land north of slavery.

Canada was not the only foreign country that blacks sought out for freedom; it was simply the only important one if measured by numbers and systematic appeal. Isolated examples have fugitive slaves fleeing to the nearest safe piece of geography, perhaps the Indian Territory, or Mexico, or the occasional spot in the Caribbean if opportunity presented itself, perhaps by stowing away on a ship. With the possible exception of Mexico, given its border with Texas, those locations were not central to the Underground Railroad.

Runaway slave notices in Texas newspapers hint at part of that story. An advertisement in a San Antonio

Harriet Beecher Stowe's attack on slavery in her 1852 novel, Uncle Tom's Cabin, *was read and acclaimed around the world. When President Abraham Lincoln was introduced to her, he supposedly said, "So you're the little woman who wrote the book that made this great war!" Stowe, top left, acknowledged the influence of the first autobiography of Josiah Henson, lower left, on her writing. Henson reached Fort Erie, Canada, in 1830 with his wife and four children. In 1841, he helped found the Dawn Settlement. Later editions of*

Henson's autobiography emphasized his connection with Uncle Tom. The Webb family, above, toured the North giving dramatic readings from Stowe's book.

Colonization in Liberia

When the American Society for Colonizing the Free People of Colour in America was established in 1816, it was looked upon with suspicion by most free blacks. Prominent politicians such as Henry Clay and John Randolph and evangelical clergymen said that Africans had been degraded in the United States, and even if slaves were emancipated, they could not rise to full citizenship. The only solution, the Society members proposed, was to offer to send free blacks to a colony in Africa where they might make their own republic. And, slaveholders added, this would tend to make slave property more secure since no African could be mistaken for a free person. It was this point that turned most free blacks away from Liberia, which the American Colonization Society had founded by 1821. Still, some blacks were attracted to Liberia as a place where they could establish their own government, develop trade and commerce, and send missionaries. In its first decade, Liberia received about 3,000 African Americans, predominately free and in families. After the early 1830s, more of the emigrants were family groups manumitted specially to be sent to Liberia. In 1847, Liberia became a republic and operated under a constitution that was modeled on—and mocked—the U.S. Constitution. By the Civil War, 14,000 black Americans had emigrated there. The emigration sparked strong emotions. Each side considered the other deluded. Although the colonization of West Africa drew more African Americans than emigrated elsewhere except for Canada, it remained unpopular among enslaved people because of its sponsorship by whites, its distance from the United States, and rumors of high death rates. Daniel Dashiel Warner (shown at right in a portrait by Thomas Sully) and his family moved to Monrovia, Liberia, in 1823 and built a shipyard. Warner served as president in 1861. The president's palace, below, looked much like houses in Maryland, Virginia, and Ohio.

paper described a man named Nelson as "probably on his way to Mexico." Dark in complexion, 6 feet tall, 160 pounds, with high cheekbones, Nelson had fled slavery well-equipped, with a Spanish horse and a fine saddle, a large double-barrel shotgun, and a "considerable sum of money." Nelson's owner promised the horse and cash to anyone who would capture the slave, "or the same reward for his scalp."

Locations outside of North America offered a powerful attraction to some African-American leaders, including fugitive slaves. Haiti, Jamaica, the West Indies, and Africa were their most common points of reference. But as destinations for the runaway slave heading out of the South, those would have been impossible goals in all but extraordinary circumstances. Such exotic foreign spots were invoked in discussions by black leaders who promoted emigration, a move out of North America, away from white-controlled nations and territories, to places where people of color made their own destiny. The argument, simply stated, was that a true black nationality could not develop and thrive in a majority white environment.

An organized effort explored an earlier African-American settlement in Liberia and emigration to Africa under the inspiration of Martin R. Delany, a physician and black nationalism's most persistent advocate. Another program sponsored several hundred blacks to settle in Haiti with disastrous results. Black leaders, fugitives among them, flirted with different locations. J.W.C. Pennington considered Jamaica briefly in the 1840s. And during the most difficult 1850s, after passage of the Fugitive Slave Law, even emigration's toughest black critics softened their objections, no longer certain that America could be reformed on matters of race and slavery.

But emigration was always more a debate among black leaders than a program for the future among black citizens. The discussion always grew fiercer in times of greatest racial troubles in the United States; but as the nation turned its attention to sectional antagonisms and finally to the Civil War, the debate grew still. Delany, emigration's wisest and most thoughtful advocate, was among the many black nationalist leaders who abandoned emigration and turned their talents to supporting the Union war effort in the hope that it would become a struggle for emancipation, America's salvation for the slaves and the oppressed.

The Underground Railroad continued throughout the Civil War and into Reconstruction. Some Southern agents, such as Harriet Tubman, became spies for the Union army while continuing to aid the growing number of runaways. Northern stations maintained their longtime functions while expanding assistance to destitute freedmen seeking shelter behind Union lines in the occupied South. After Abraham Lincoln issued the Emancipation Proclamation in 1863, tens of thousands of slaves left plantations in Confederate territory to join a passing Union column or made their way to a federal army encampment, where they often were turned away or welcomed with less than a liberator's embrace.

As the war drew to a close and the nation faced the pressing question about the future of the freed slaves, the underground network shifted its focus to relief efforts, collecting funds, food, and clothing for those who left bondage with little more than the clothes they were wearing. The network that for so long waged an active war against slavery turned its attention in peacetime to helping define the terms of emancipation.

With the end of Reconstruction and the passing of time, the Underground Railroad has been elevated to the place of national legend, its status earned by sacrifices in the campaign against tyranny and conferred as the embodiment of the nation's foremost principles of freedom and liberty.

On foot, on horseback, in wagons, any way they could, slaves in increasing numbers fled to Union lines as Federal armies invaded different parts of the South. The North declared the runaways contraband and gave them food and shelter and put them to work preparing meals, digging trenches, and other troop support activities.

This painting of Mulberry Plantation in South Carolina by an unknown artist shows the slave quarters located close to the main residence.

In 1832, William Lloyd Garrison and 10 fellow abolitionists founded the New England Anti-Slavery Society at the African Meeting House in Boston. This photograph shows the church in 1875.

Recognizing Historic Places

Many sites in the United States are said to be associated with the Underground Railroad. Some of these may be eligible for listing in the National Register of Historic Places. Definitively deciding which ones were "stations" on or otherwise related to the informal network of slave-escape routes is difficult, because, as Larry Gara points out in the introduction to this book, many aspects of the Underground Railroad story have taken on a mythical aura.

The National Register of Historic Places, administered by the National Park Service under the Secretary of the Interior, is the official list of the nation's cultural districts, sites, buildings, structures, and objects that are significant in American history, architecture, archeology, engineering, and culture. These resources contribute to an understanding of the historical and cultural foundations of the nation.

Most nominations to the National Register are made by the states through State Historic Preservation Offices (SHPO). State review boards, composed of professionals in the fields of American history, architectural history, architecture, prehistoric and historic archeology, and other related disciplines make recommendations to the SHPO when a nomination meets the National Register criteria and should be forwarded to the National Park Service.

The Secretary of the Interior also is responsible for determining which properties have national significance to all Americans and therefore may be designated as National Historic Landmarks. The National Park Service, which also administers the National Historic Landmarks Program, works with other governmental agencies and private organizations in studying places and nominating them for designation as Landmarks.

Initial requests for consideration may come from organizations, SHPOs, local officials, or owners. The National Park System Advisory Board, composed of citizens appointed by the Secretary, reviews nominations to determine whether a property meets the Landmark criteria and then conveys its recommendations to the Secretary, who makes the final decision about Landmark designation.

Listing in the National Register does not interfere with a private property owner's right to alter, manage, or dispose of the property. Owners of properties designated as Landmarks also do not give up any rights of ownership or use. Because a federal agency must consider the effects of a proposed project on a property listed in or eligible for listing in the National Register, including National Historic Landmarks, the listing may help protect the historic place against possible adverse threats from federal projects, such as highways or utility lines.

National Register listing and Landmark designation also may make the owner eligible for certain tax incentives and preservation grants. Pending legislation requires the National Park Service to create an official, uniform symbol or device which will mark all historic properties associated with the Underground Railroad listed in the National Register.

Verification: Documents and Artifacts

The Rokeby Museum and Fort Mose are associated with the story of runaways and illustrate how historians use evidence ranging from archeological excavations and site inspections to documents and aerial photography to verify a site's significance. Both are National Historic Landmarks.

Rokeby, in Ferrisburgh, Vermont, was the home and farmstead of the Robinson family, 1793 to 1961. Thomas Robinson was an active member of state and local antislavery

societies, but it was his son, Rowland Thomas Robinson, right, who became an ardent abolitionist and sheltered fugitives. The family's help to runaways is well documented in the museum's collection of 10,000 documents. They include letters from abolitionists Lucretia Mott and William Lloyd Garrison. Other letters concern the safety and job prospects of fugitives, along with documentation of one slaveholder's attempts to get a fugitive to return voluntarily. The papers reveal that some runaways were given temporary shelter while others stayed there to work.

Fort Mose, labeled simply as "Negroe Fort" on the map at left, dates to the era when Spain controlled Florida and fought with England over the lands around Florida's present border with Georgia. Africans and Indians crossed the border into Florida to escape enslavement or extinction under the English. In 1738 Florida offered sanctuary to fugitive slaves and made them part of a militia. To increase defenses and to house the blacks, the Spaniards established a town and fort two miles to the north called Gracia Real de Santa Teresa de Mose. The fort and a subsequent fort were used until 1763 when Spain ceded Florida to England. In 1976 Jack Williams believed he had located the site of Fort Mose in a salt marsh he owned. Ten years later the Florida Museum of Natural History began a study of the site. With the help of the National Aeronautics and Space Administration, archeologists used thermal images to determine the now-underwater site of the first fort and used maps, plus aerial photographs and archeological excavations to locate the second fort on a small island in the marsh. From documents in Spain, Florida, and other places and from bones, seeds, and artifacts, they are putting together the story of Fort Mose, which is administered by the Florida Department of Environmental Protection.

Further Reading

By Marie Tyler-McGraw

At the core of the Underground Railroad story is an argument about the nature of American slavery and the extent to which enslaved African Americans could and did carry out their own plans for escape.

Many American historians writing in the late 19th and early 20th centuries characterized the slave system as benign and the slaves as content. To do this, they had to minimize the importance of runaways. U.B. Phillips's book, *American Negro Slavery* (New York: D. Appleton, 1918), was the culmination of this work and dominated the field for decades. Phillips portrayed escape from bondage as insignificant to the history of slavery.

It was not until the 1950s that mainstream historians began to review the documentary evidence and came to conclusions that interpreted slavery and the slave quite differently. Works by Kenneth Stampp, *The Peculiar Institution* (New York: Vintage Press, 1956) and Stanley Elkins, *Slavery: A Problem in American Institutional and Intellectual Life* (Chicago: University of Chicago Press, 1959) saw slavery as harsh, and, in Elkins's case, as robbing the enslaved of their sense of self.

These two books sparked a generation of research beginning in the 1960s that examined every aspect of the system of slavery and generally concluded that slavery, although deeply damaging to the African American, did not destroy the possibility of independent thought and action. The Underground Railroad, already the subject of some histories and memoirs and a part of many local legends, was reexamined as a slave-directed enterprise.

Many of the local legends gathered in the late 19th century were published as oral histories, memoirs, newspaper articles, and other memorabilia of the Underground Railroad. They were primarily collected by those sympathetic to abolitionism. The most important collected primary sources from that era are Wilbur Siebert, *The Underground Railway from Slavery to Freedom* (New York: The Macmillan Company, 1898) and William Still, *The Underground Railroad* (reprint edition Arno Press: New York, 1968; original edition Philadelphia, 1872). Siebert gathered documents and reminiscences from aged abolitionists or their descendants in the 1890s. Still, an active participant in the Philadelphia Underground Railroad, attempted after the Civil War to reconstruct each narrative for publication.

More contemporary are C. Peter Ripley, et al., editors, *The Black Abolitionist Papers,* five volumes (Chapel Hill: University of North Carolina Press, 1985-93) and Charles Blockson, *The Underground Railroad* (New York: Prentice Hall, 1987).

A classic work on black history is John Hope Franklin and Alfred Moss Jr., *From Slavery to Freedom: A History of African Americans* (7th ed., New York: McGraw Hill Publishing Co., 1994).

The best examination of evidence done thus far to separate the myth from the reality of the Underground Railroad is Larry Gara's *The Liberty Line: The Legend of the Underground Railroad* (reprint edition Lexington: University Press of Kentucky; 1996; original edition Lexington, 1961). His first and last chapters are an account of exaggerated and romanticized texts and newspaper accounts. Gara has performed the central historical task of asking what evidence exists, and he provides a good list of fictionalized citations to avoid.

Since Gara's book was written, the 1930s Works Progress Administration (WPA) oral histories of slavery and the fugitive slave memoirs of the late antebellum era from 1830 to 1860 have been combed for references to runaways and the Underground Railroad. Most of the accounts of slave narratives published since 1970—such as John Blassingame's *Slave Testimony: Two Centuries of Letters, Speeches, Interviews and Autobiographies* (Baton Rouge: Louisiana University Press, 1977) and George Rawick, *From Sundown to Sunup: The Making of a Black Community* (Westport, Connecticut: Greenwood Press, 1972)—have come from those sources.

Useful sources for analyzing fugitive slave memoirs include Gilbert Osofsky, editor, *Puttin' on Ole Massa* (New York: Harper Torchbooks, 1969); Robin Winks, *The Blacks in Canada* (New Haven: Yale, 1971); Charles T. Davis and Henry Louis Gates, Jr., editors, *The Slave's Narrative* (New York: Oxford University Press, 1985); and R.J.M. Blackett, *Beating Against the Barriers: Biographical Essays in Nineteenth-Century Afro-American History* (Baton Rouge: Louisiana State University Press, 1986). They note which fugitive memoirs were written by the fugitive, which were told to an editor or amanuensis, which were edited much later, which were entirely false, and which were changed substantially between one edition and the other.

An excellent place to begin the history of antislavery in North America is Merton Dillon, *Slavery Attacked: Southern Slaves and Their Allies, 1619-1865* (Baton Rouge: Louisiana State University Press, 1990). Overviews of the abolitionists may be found in James Stewart, *Holy Warriors: The Abolitionists and American Slavery* (New York: Hill and Wang, 1976) and Benjamin Quarles, *Black Abolitionists* (New York: Oxford University Press, 1969).

The best summary of the philosophical development of antislavery in the Western tradition is David Brion Davis, *Slavery and Human Progress* (New York: Oxford University Press, 1984). Thomas Haskell makes the argument for the relation between benevolence and a prospering economy in "Capitalism and the Origins of the Humanitarian Sensibility," *American Historical Review* 90, nos. 3 and 4, (April and June, 1985).

The religious impulse in antislavery usually begins in the mid-18th century with the Society of Friends, or Quakers, in England and America who began to view slavery as an evil. Although Quakers were not the only religious group to oppose slavery, they became the best known. For an account of their spiritual journey, see Jean Soderlund, *Quakers and Slavery: A Divided Spirit* (Princeton: Princeton University Press, 1985).

The religious debate over slavery caused denominational divisions and the development of Biblical arguments for and against slavery. The rise of evangelical Protestantism at the same time as Enlightenment-based arguments for American independence and liberty are explored in such books as Rhys Isaac, *The Transformation of Virginia, 1744-1790* (Chapel Hill: University of North Carolina Press for Williamsburg, Virginia: The Institute of Early American History and Culture, 1982). Three excellent books on the development of a black theology and cosmos rooted in both Christianity and slavery are Albert Raboteau, *Slave Religion: The Invisible Institution* (New York: Oxford University Press. 1978); Mechal Sobel, *Trabelin'*

On: The Slave Journey to an Afro-Baptist Faith (Westport, Connecticut: Greenwood Press, 1979); and Eugene Genovese, Roll, Jordan, Roll: The World the Slaves Made (New York: Pantheon Books, 1974).

The Journal of Negro History, which began publication in 1916 under the editorship of Carter G. Woodson, often provided a venue for the publication of excellent scholarship on African-American life in the decades before 1970 when the official American history journals were almost closed to that subject.

Useful overviews of the changing interpretations of slavery and of black life in the South include Peter Kolchin, American Slavery: 1619-1877 (New York: Hill and Wang, 1993) and Peter Parish, Slavery: History and Historians (New York: Harper and Row, 1989).

For the life of Northern free blacks, see Chapter 3, "Links to Bondage," in James Oliver Horton, Free People of Color: Inside the African-American Community (Washington: Smithsonian Institution Press, 1993) and James Oliver Horton and Lois E. Horton, In Hope of Liberty (New York: Oxford University Press, 1997).

John W. Blassingame, The Slave Community: Plantation Life in the Antebellum South (New York: Oxford University Press, 1972) argues that slaves were able to overcome many of the obstacles that were designed to keep them separate from each other and dependent on the masters, as does Herbert G. Gutman, The Black Family in Slavery and Freedom, 1750-1925 (New York: Vintage Books, 1976). For a recent analysis of the slave family, see Brenda E. Stevenson, Life in Black and White:

Family and Community in the Slave South (New York: Oxford University Press, 1996).

Slave insurrection and rebellion, often betrayed before they began, were never successful in the United States. Herbert Aptheker's American Negro Slave Revolts (New York: International Publishers, 1943) is often criticized for his tendency to accept all evidence for slave revolt, but the book is comprehensive. Douglas Egerton has written Gabriel's Rebellion (Chapel Hill: University of North Carolina Press, 1993), and Stephen Oates has written of Nat Turner in The Fires of Jubilee (New York: Harper & Row, 1975; Perennial Library Edition, 1990). See also Peter Wood, Black Majority: Negroes in Colonial South Carolina from 1670 Through the Stono Rebellion (New York: Knopf, 1974).

David Walker's Appeal, an angry and eloquent indictment of slavery by a black man whose writing influenced Northern antislavery and Southern reactions, is available in several editions. See Herbert Aptheker, editor, One Continual Cry: David Walker's Appeal to the Colored Citizens of the World (1829-1830): Its Setting, Its Meaning (New York: Humanities Press, 1965) or Peter P. Hinks, To Awaken My Afflicted Brethren: David Walker and the Problem of Antebellum Slave Resistance (University Park, Pa.: Pennsylvania State University Press, 1997).

The creation and persistence of African-American cultural identity are discussed in Lawrence Levine, Black Culture and Black Consciousness: Afro-American Thought from Slavery to Freedom (New York: Oxford University Press, 1977), and the origins of pan-African nationalism are the topic of Floyd J. Miller, The Search for a Black Nationality: Black

Emigration and Colonization, 1787-1863 (Urbana: University of Illinois Press, 1975).

For life in Canada, see Robin Winks, *The Blacks in Canada* (New Haven: Yale University Press, 1971); Michael Wayne, "The Black Population of Canada West on the Eve of the American Civil War: A Reassessment Based on the Manuscript Census of 1861," *Social History,* Volume 28, no. 56 (November 1995); and Gary Collison, *Shadrach Minkins: From Fugitive Slave to Citizen* (Cambridge, Massachusetts: Harvard University Press, 1997).

For Mexico and the Southwest, see Randolph Campbell. *An Empire for Liberty: The Peculiar Institution in Texas, 1821-1865* (Baton Rouge: Louisiana State University Press, 1989).

For the travel journal of an abolitionist who went to Mexico, Canada, and Haiti seeking the best accommodations for free blacks, read Benjamin Earle, editor, *Life, Travels and Opinions of Benjamin Lundy* (reprint edition New York: Arno Press, 1969). Also see Kenneth Mulroy, *Freedom on the Border: The Seminole Maroons in Florida, the Indian Territory, Coahuila, and Texas* (Lubbock: Texas Tech University Press, 1993).

Other Titles

Here are a few other publications suggested by Larry Gara, Brenda E. Stevenson, and C. Peter Ripley:

- Arna W. Bontemps, editor, *Five Black Lives: The Autobiographies of Venture Smith, James Mars, William Grimes, The Rev. G.W. Offley and James L. Smith* (Middletown: Wesleyan University Press, 1971).
- Nat Brandt, *The Town That Started the Civil War* (Syracuse: Syracuse University Press, 1990).
- Philip S. Foner, *History of Black Americans: From the Emergence of the Cotton Kingdom to the Eve of the Compromise of 1850* (Westport, Connecticut: Greenwood Press, 1983).
- Byron D. Fruehling and Robert H. Smith, "Subterranean Hideaways of the Underground Railroad in Ohio: An Architectural and Historical Critique of Local Tradition," *Ohio History* 102 (1993): 98-117.
- James Oliver Horton and Lois E. Horton, *Black Bostonians: Family Life and Community Struggle in the Antebellum North* (New York: Holmes & Meier, 1979).
- Carol Kammen, *On Doing Local History: Reflections on What Local Historians Do, Why, and What It Means* (Walnut Creek, California: Alta Mira Press, for Nashville, Tennessee: American Association for State and Local History, 1986).
- David E. Kyvig and Myron A. Marty, *Nearby History: Exploring the Past Around You* (Walnut Creek, California: Alta Mira Press, 1996; first edition, American Association for State and Local History, 1982).
- Stephen B. Oates, editor, and John S. Ford, *Rip Ford's Texas* (Austin: University of Texas Press, 1963).
- Joe M. Richardson, editor, *Trial and Imprisonment of Jonathan Walker at Pensacola, Florida: Aiding Slaves to Escape From Bondage* (Gainesville: University Presses of Florida, 1974).
- Stuart S. Sprague, editor, *His Promised Land: The Autobiography of John P. Parker, Former Slave and Conductor on the Underground Railroad* (New York: W.W. Norton & Co., 1996).
- Julie Winch, *Philadelphia's Black Elite: Activism, Accommodation, and the Struggle for Autonomy, 1787-1848* (Philadelphia: Temple University Press, 1988).

Index

This handbook may be purchased by mail from the Superintendent of Documents, U.S. Government Printing Office, Washington, D.C. 20402-9325.

☆GPO:1998—433-620/60508 Reprint 1998 Printed on recycled paper.

87

National Park Service

Picture Sources

Most photographs and illustrations credited below are restricted against commercial reproduction. Abbreviations: LC—Library of Congress; NA—National Archives; NPS—National Park Service; NYHS—New-York Historical Society; SCRBC—Schomburg Center for Research in Black Culture, New York Public Library.

Front cover ©Jerry Pinkney; inside front cover SCRBC; 2-3 Mark N. Mueller, M.D.; 4-5 Brooklyn Museum of Art; 6 Addison Thompson; 9 Dave Gilbert; 10 Joanne Devereaux; 11 Free Library of Philadelphia; 13 Mae Scanlan; 14 *branding* SCRBC, *Constitution* NA, *"Boston Massacre"* Boston Athenaeum, *Douglass* J.R. Eyerman, Life Magazine © Time, Inc.; *Tubman* LC; 15 *book ad* NYHS, *soldiers* LC; 15 John Brown, *Lincoln* LC, *Dred Scott* Missouri Historical Society; 16-17 ©Jerry Pinkney; 18, 19 Stratford Historical Society; 20-21 *map* NPS; 20 *bust* Metropolitan Museum of Art; 21 *slave* Musee de L'Homme; *ship* Mariners' Museum, Newport News, Va.; 22 *branding* SCRBC, *bell harness, brand* NPS; 23 *slave* NA; 24 *Equiano* Bridgeman Art Library, London; 24 *huddled boys* Mansell, Time, Inc.; 25 Library Company of Philadelphia; 28-29 Turner Stock Montage; 28 *"Tragical Scene"* Virginia Historical Society; 29 *Amistad, Cinque* New Haven Colony Historical Society; 31 *porter tag* American Numismatics Society, *other tags* Charleston Museum, S.C.; 32-33 *painting* ©Jerry Pinkney; 32 *nursemaid* Louisiana State Museum, *field hands* Corbis-Bettmann; 34 *slave quarters* Lightfoot Collection, *burial* Historic New Orleans Collection; 35 Blue Ridge Institute and Museums; 36-37 *map* NPS; 36 *almanac* Maryland Historical Society, *Isaac Jefferson* University of Virginia; 37 *Molineux* National Portrait Gallery, *tag* American Numismatics Society, *woman* George Eastman House; 40 SCRBC; 41 Heinz Family Office; 42 *family* LC, *wedding* North Carolina Museum of Art; 44 LC; 46, 47 SCRBC; 48-49 *"Slave Hunt"* Philbrook Museum of Art; 48 *"$150 Reward"* LC; 49 *Henry Brown* Granger Collection, *map* NPS; 50 *map* NPS; 51 American Antiquarian Society; 53 *Douglass* J.R. Eyerman, Life Magazine © Time, Inc., *"North Star"* SCRBC; 55 *portraits* SCRBC, *title page* NPS; 56-57 *rescuers* Oberlin College; 56 *"No Union"* SCRBC; 57 *convention* Madison County Historical Society, N.Y., *"The Liberator," "Anti-Slave-Catchers"* SCRBC; 58 LC; 59 NPS; 60 Cincinnati Art Museum; 62 SCRBC; 63 Massachusetts Historical Society; 64-65 *contrabands* NYHS; 65 *soldiers* Chicago Historical Society, *"Colored Soldiers!"* NPS; 66 NA; 67 Larry Sherer ©Time, Inc.; 68 SCRBC; 69 *Elgin* Archives of Ontario, *"Stockholders"* SCRBC; 70 *Stowe, Henson* SCRBC, *ad* NYHS; 71 Harriet Beecher Stowe Center; 72 *Monrovia* LC, *portrait* Historical Society of Pennsylvania; 74 NA; 76-77 Gibbes Museum of Art; 78 Society for the Preservation of New England Antiquities; 80 Rokeby Museum, Vt.; 81 Florida Museum of Natural History; back cover *Milton House* Addison Thompson, *tag* American Numismatics Society; *Douglass* J.R. Eyerman, Life Magazine © Time, Inc., *Tubman* LC.